Frankie Goes to Portugal

Frankie Shanley/Regan

CONTENTS

1. Protection Duty.

It was 9pm in a bar in Letterfrack Connemara. It was a dimly lit cosy bar with a lovely smell of turf coming from the stack beside the fire. I was constantly monitoring the crowd, looking at everyone trying to read them and gauge their attitudes as they looked at our table. Some were clearly not happy with our presence and they were now starting to make it clear. I was on unofficial protection duty. The travelling District Court Judge was staying in the B&B upstairs and wanted to come for a quiet drink in the bar. He had heard that there was a Garda (Irish Police Officer) also staying in the B&B and had asked the owner if i would sit beside him in the bar for an hour, i agreed. The word had got around and some customers weren't happy that we were there.

I had to remain calm and show my authority and so i walked up to the bar in between them and in a loud articulate voice ordered another round for me and the Judge, yes, i could have done same at the table but it was a psychological move to show them i wasn't intimidated and it seemed to work as the comments stopped and they changed conversation. It was a little trick that's taught in Templemore in Ireland (where Irish Police are trained). I sat back down with the Judge and we spoke for ages, he was a lovely man and extremely intelligent. He had asked me if i had any cases before him and i said no and that seemed to put him at ease. We spoke about everyday things and then literature, GAA and life and after an hour we were like friends, by now the bar had resumed to normality with the excitement of our being there now long gone.

I had often wondered abut what kind of life a judge had, it must be hard making all those decisions and not being able to go anywhere in public for fear of meeting a relative or friend of someone he/she had given a Prison Sentence to. Our conversation changed to me and my "career" and so i opened up to him, i explained to him how the job was starting to get to me, the pressures were immense and i was starting to bring it home with me. He seemed genuinely concerned and gave me some great advice that night as we sat by the fire which i remember to this day. After another hour or so he decided to call it a night as he was "On the bench" in the morning in Clifden and so i walked him to his room and we parted ways, i had a quick look around to make sure no- one had seen what room he was in and was confident all was okay.

I went back to the bar and sat by the fire with my drink thinking about the advice i was just given by the Judge. I suddenly became overwhelmed with emotion. I started to think about my Girl who was home alone and struggling emotionally and god how i missed her and wished life could be normal for us both. I thought about all the mistakes i had made in the recent past and felt my eyes getting teary. This was now a big problem as i couldn't let anyone see my emotions. I pretended my phone was vibrating in my pocket and pretended to answer it "Hang on it's hard to hear you" i said while standing up and walking to the front door to go outside whilst avoiding the "How are you Garda" from the locals smoking outside. I got in the car and drove to a quiet pier in Leenane (i only had 2 drinks) and I sat there in the car listening to Kc and Jo Jo's "All my life" it was our song, i thought again about how much i missed her and burst into tears. What was i doing! What the F$£k was i doing! Not a normal reaction for a Garda you might say, but there was much more going on then you know. You see, i wasn't a Garda, i had booked into the B&B

earlier and in conversion after insinuated that i was a Garda, i had done that as people wouldn't ask me too many questions and they would leave me alone, if they thought they had recognised me from somewhere before they would have assumed it was whilst i was working. I was in fact "On the Run' from the law. and my picture had been on most News Papers for weeks.

This is my story

2. A Shiny Mercedes

It was a beautiful red Mercedes Benz, i had driven past the Garage and noticed it straight away at the front. I drove back to the Garage and had a quick look around it. I was approached by a Salesman and we chatted for some time before he threw me the keys and said

"Take it for a test drive" and that's when everything went downhill! I gave him the keys to my BMW and drove out of the showroom and kept the car for 4 days. It made me feel important to be seen in it, i was getting noticed which made me feel good and for a moment took my depression away. You see, i had done this almost 7 times by now and the Car i had just given the salesman i had taken from a test drive a few days previously in another part of Ireland. I pulled over and posted a letter to the salesman apologising for my actions and telling him where his car now was before phoning the local Garda station and telling them the same thing. I was deeply depressed, i mean deeply deeply depressed. It was the lowest anyone could feel, i was always crying and didn't want to be around people. When i had a New Car on a test drive it was giving me (albeit short lived) a moment of Joy and emotion which was literally keeping me going, it's hard to explain to anyone who hasn't suffered from it.

One thing about depression is that it somehow manifests itself in strange ways and affects everyone differently. Life was hard, I was staying in holiday homes and sleeping in the cars. When i would book a holiday home i would book it at the last minute for a week and would always arrive late at night. That way the key would be left out for me and i wouldn't have to see or interact with anyone.

The nights were hard, i always found it so hard to sleep, every sound i heard would wake me no matter how low it was, i would get up and walk around the house for hours checking things and looking out the window from paranoia. I was supposed to be on medication for sleeping and depression but was afraid to reach out to any doctor as by now my Picture was appearing in Newspapers in

Ireland with the over the top headline "Catch him if you can". They were likening me to the character in the Movie staring Leonardo De Caprio and at this stage i was being accused of crimes i wasn't committing. There were reports from "Sources" in the Gardai saying that i was responsible for crimes that obviously could not have been me as i was in the opposite end of the country at the time and so my fake persona was now starting to snowball.

From the age of 16 i had started to get depressed, at that time it was something that was not spoken about and when your 16 and you have it it's worse, i isolated myself from everyone including my family and would not leave my bedroom for the fear of having to interact with anyone.

I was living with my Granny, her husband (Grandad) has passed away and I was there for company growing up. My parents are great, it was the summer of 1990 and they had bought me a Cassette deck which at the time was state of the art, now it wouldn't look out of place in a museum. That was the moment that changed my life forever, they hadn't given me just a cassette deck, but the gift of Music. Music is one of the most powerful things in the World, it can take you right back in time and help you relive any moment right down to the sights and smells at that exact time. It can open emotions in an instant and can be comforting at any time.

For me that's what it was, comforting. I would spend night after night listening to Radio 3 in Tullamore and Shannonside (my local station) 2FM and Atlantic 252 and be amazed at the Dj's and how they could make you feel as if it was you they were just talking to you. I would start to record songs and i started to build a collection and it was keeping me going and more importantly keeping me focused. Every now and then ye old depression would come back and hit me hard and i would go for a walk alone at 3 or 4am in my home town of Boyle to take my mind of it. I wouldn't see anyone, as i didn't want too, I loved Boyle at night, it was beautiful and comforting like an old friend, the Abbey at night, the Pleasure Grounds, so many wonderful places in a pretty little town, and no people. At this stage I had been hospitalised 2 times at the ages of 17 over suicide attempts. The Health System was different back then, you would arrive at the Hospital clearly in serious distress and yet you would be sent home the following day.

I feel now i can say this to you as I want to be open in every way in this book no matter how embarrassing it is for me. In my early 20's i spent them in a care facility with elderly people. It was a recommendation from my Doctors and to be honest I strangely liked it, I felt at ease around people who wouldn't judge you and we would spend days watching TV and other tasks to keep our minds occupied. Looking back now I feel so sorry for my family for my putting them through all of this.

3. Tony Fenton

Listening to those Dj's was my release, I was enthralled with how they would stop speaking the milli second the Music stopped and one in particular was Tony Fenton. Tony presented a Radio Show on 2FM called the Hotline and it was the highlight of my day, he would play new music and the big songs of the day in 60minutes while interviewing the artists themselves. He had background music while he was speaking and the jingles were so fast and slick. I then decided to try it myself and so made a very basic studio. At 2am after "Moloney after Midnight" (big show in the 90's) i would start my own show, i had recorded Jingles and music and would introduce the song like Tony did, now I was rubbish to be fair but practice makes perfect and so would pretend to be live every night from 2am-6am 7 nights a week. Sleep?

Sleep was now at the stage when i would just collapse from tiredness. Eventually I started to get better on my made up Radio Show, my vocals seemed to be getting more polished and more importantly my timing was almost done to perfection at the age of 18. I had made a friend back then who was our local Dj, a wonderful man from Boyle called DJ Dermot, Dermot not only was a genius when it came to all things Music but he was also a good friend.

The first Disco i went to was when I was 17 and it was in St Joseph's Hall in Boyle. It was (still is) a large rectangular shape which was an acoustical nightmare for any band/DJ. When i went to the disco I sat down in the corner just waiting to go home but had been persuaded by my family to go with my cousin Timmy. The Music was low when I arrived, disco lights were flashing and it didn't have any effect on me. Then Dermot came on the Mic and said hello in his friendly Dj Voice and welcomed us all, then BOOM Full Volume, the Water boys "the whole of the moon" came on, everyone screamed in excitement and the hairs stood up on the back of my neck, This is what I was going to do.

Through talking to Dermot he knew I was interested and he started to help me, I would go to gigs with him, I was always listening and watching him and gauging the reaction of the crowd, he knew when it was dropping and always knew what to do to pick them up, he was a master at his craft. He then introduced me to Pirate Radio, Atlantis 94Q which he broadcast from a shed on FM around Boyle, it was amazing and he would teach me how to do a show and get my vocals on point.

In 1994 RTE 2FM (national radio) launched the famous "DJ For a Day" competition on the Hotline with Tony Fenton which was huge back then and launched most of Ireland's big Radio Dj's. Nowadays in Ireland it's all about the "Click" if your just out of college or on TV or know the owner you'll get a radio gig. Back then it had to be in your blood and you had to be at it for years and have a Radio Personality. Dermot persuaded me to enter the Dj for a Day Competition. I was hesitant but tried it for the laugh, i recorded myself in his shed introducing a track and sent it (post back then) to RTE.

It was a Friday evening and I was at home in my room recording Music when my granny entered the room and told me "there's someone on the phone for you" I brought the phone into my room and a big voice aid to me "Frankie my man, Tony Fenton here" Jesus, as i'm typing this i'm getting goosebumps, this was huge, Tony was on the phone talking to me! He told me my demo was so cool and that i was selected as the final 20 and through to the next round. He would call me next Wednesday at 7:10pm live on the Hotline and i would have to introduce Sister Sledge's "We are family". To say I was excited as an understatement. The following day people were ringing me congratulating me and i had a small taste of fame which made me extremely uncomfortable. That weekend I practiced and practiced and practiced. Monday 6pm the phone rang, it was an RTE Producer, one of the contestants had backed out and they were stuck and wanted to know would I do my piece today instead, i agreed and rang everyone i knew to tell them i was on air that night. 7:10pm came and I went On- Air and the following day it was the big conversation in school.

School was hard, people were trying to talk to me but I was always stand offish and probably seemed weird to everyone, there were great moments though, the likes of Mr Tivnan my English teacher i owe so much to. He knew that i was a good reader and speaker and would make me read stories aloud to the class everyday, he knew what he was doing, I was getting more confident at public speaking and more forceful and was starting to get a flair for story telling. Another teacher of mine Mr Conboy was just so wonderful in every way, he could read a story like Robin Williams in the Dead Poets Society and would act it out with us while jumping on a table and just making us all laugh and love history, wonderful wonderful times looking back.

Friday evening RTE called me live On-

Air on the Hotline, I was now through to the final 10! The next step was to come to RTE in Dublin, I had to Co-Present the Hotline with Tony and do a live gig somewhere in Swords in front of the Hotpress Music Magazine and RTE judges. I got the bus to Dublin from the Royal Hotel in Boyle and made the long journey to Dublin, I was so excited and yet nervous at the same time. Tony collected me from my Hotel in Donnybrook in a big cream Mercedes and was as cool in real life as he was on the Radio. He drove me to the studios the long way so he could talk to me and you know what, we connected. Not in the "He had to be nice" level, but a deeper one, i told him of my depression and life and he told me about him growing up in Dublin, he told me life is too short and gave me his personal mobile number for to call him if i ever got low again. He was now a friend.

We got to the Studios and Tony was

like a master on-air, he was slick, fast and super cool all at the same time. Effortless! My turn came to talk and to be fair i was rubbish! It was all eh eh and yes and no and no conversation and my intros were off, but he kept me focused and had his arm on my shoulder telling me take a breath and relax. The fact that I was on National Radio was starting to seep into my mind and everything was starting to unravel for me. We went to the live gig which I remember to this day, he spoke to me on the way there and gave me tips, he said "feed off their energy" He went on first and had them eating out of the palm of his hands, then he introduced me and man i was good! I was full of energy, was laughing and joking with them, on a big empty stage, just me and a club filled with screaming teenagers. I loved it! Tony was also excited that i had gone from struggling in the Studio to being a different person on stage just 2 hours later. It was an amazing experience and for those few hours i felt on top of the world.

4. I think i Peed on Jon Bon Jovi

We drove around Dublin City for an hour, he showed me all the sights and said he loved Dublin City at night. We spoke more and it was clear now that he was trying to help me with what was going on in my life and that he liked me. Whilst in the car his carphone rang and he answered on speaker, it was Gabrielle! The singer, who sang "Dreams" he told her to say hi to me and she did, this was mind blowing now! After some time we stopped and started to walk down Grafton Street. For me this was a dream, I was in the capital with Tony Fenton living my Radio dream and loving every second of it. We walked to a Club where we were whisked passed the queue and into

Lilly's Bordello, the hub of fame in the 90's in Ireland! It was there I met the very talented John Kenny, a fantastic broadcaster and a nice man too, we shook hands as had seen each other through the Studio glass on the Hotline as John was reading the Sport before the Hotline aired.

John has been a constant supporter of mine for some time now, when i launched my own station in 2005 he joined it (more on that later) and has been a good friend on Social media since then and to this day.

We all spoke for hours in the library in the Bordello, i was recognizing so many people from TV and whilst I wanted to go say hi I was too shy. Tony introduced me to so many people as his buddy, he was such a nice guy. After some time I had the urge to go to the bathroom and after getting directions went there, on the way I was passing celebrities from TV and some of the

Singers i was playing earlier on 2FM. I went to the gents bathroom and stood there whilst (ahem) doing my thing, I was reading a Newspaper article in front of me on the wall and got slightly disorientated and moved a bit to the left when i heard an American accent say "Whoa Dude". I apologized and looked at the person and froze, it was Jon Bon Jovi! They were playing in Dublin that week. Yes, I froze, but my bodily functions had other ideas and his reaction said he wasn't impressed. Yes I ever so slightly peed on Jon Bon Jovi. I went back to Tony and told him what happened and he loved it, we laughed for ages and spoke again about life, he really was trying to help me.

He drove me back to my hotel and I slept soundly after what was the strangest night of my life. I went back to Boyle and normality kicked in, back to my room at night alone presenting a fake radio show that didn't exist after my experience of a lifetime in Dublin. My old foe Depression came back harder than ever now.

I received another call from RTE to say that i was now in the final 5 of the National Dj Competition. Everyone was now talking about it and i was in the National Papers and on TV. I went to Dublin with my friend Jonathan and arrived at Club M in Dublin for the final. The final 5 had to Dj in the Club. I was rubbish, i was less than rubbish, i was scared, i was afraid to look anyone in the eye, my depression was back and i did not want to be here. East 17's House of Love was big the time and the Stereo Mc's Creation, great songs for Radio, but not a club. I was learning the hard way.

Another Frankie from Mayo won the competition which nearly gave me heart failure when the first name was mentioned and he deserved it, recently we've become friends on Facebook and it was very hard for me to send him the request as i know people have heard and read a lot about me over the years that hasn't been true. I went back to Boyle to my room, i turned off the lights, the LED's from my little studio were like Christmas decorations calling me back and i went back to my Fake Radio hosting. I was hospitalised again shortly after but this time they kept me for a few days.

I don't remember much of it, and I'm glad I don't.

I know that i cried a lot and that was when a sad part of my life started. Crying became the norm, and for no reason. I stayed in bed and didn't want to talk to anyone including my family.

When i would eventually tell someone about my experience with what happened with Tony and Jon Bon Jovi and my gig in front of all the teens and being on National Radio, i wasn't believed because after all i was on medication..

...and weird.

I've typed the last few lines like that for a reason, i want to slow you all down to a stop, because now life was about to take a bad turn. I'm not an author, damn they are talented. I'm just gonna do my best and apologise in advance if you're expecting a literary work of art.

5. A Shining Light

The next few years came and went, by now i had given up on my radio dream and was traveling the country and getting in trouble for small things. I was working as a Red Coat in Mosney

Holiday Centre, the Irish Butlins. I was well liked, there were moment of normality and for a while the depression lifted, and now, I was making friends.

It was Sunday night in Mosney, I was due to start Djing at the club there. Shakers was the name of the nightclub and i had stumbled into the gig by accident. I started as a Red Coat but it was soon evident that i was good on the Microphone and so i was given some gigs in the club I couldn't move from the bed, the depression just hit me hard like a train. I could hear people knocking at the door asking was I okay, and back then depression was something no-one spoke about. I was the fun DJ everyone knew, i couldn't let people see me cry for no reason, Eventually the door was forced open and at this stage I was crying in the bed. My boss asked me what was wrong, at the time I didn't want to tell him, I couldn't, so i told him 2 friends had died in a car accident. He was a good man, and told me to take the night off and that made me feel worse knowing I had lied. I have great memories of Mosney Holiday Camp and that man who sadly passed away young a few years later.

I would never want to go home to Roscommon because of paranoia and still thinking now that everyone was laughing at me over what happened back then (even though they weren't). I had worked on a local Radio Station presenting the Golden hour thanks to a good station owner at the time, but to be fair i wasn't ready for it, i was too young and in a bad place. I remember mobile phones had just come in and i was one of the first to have one as i love technology. I was leaving the Radio Studio in Longford and took a call walking up the lane from someone. As i was talking on the phone i heard a serious of bleeps, it was call waiting and so i answered it, all i heard were people laughing at me calling me names.

One of the guys at the station had called me in front of everyone else saying that i was pretending to be on the phone. When i answered it seemed like he was right, back then if you didn't have a mobile you didn't know that Call Waiting existed. I was humiliated and shortly after left the station. In 1999 i applied for a job on a Clare station and was giving the Saturday night show which picked me up and gave me a new lease on life. Man I loved it!

I finished my radio show from the studios in Clare and started the long journey to Galway, my Cousin was with me and the thrill of leaving a Radio Show to travel to a gig on a Saturday night had kicked in. At that time i had a blue Ford Mondeo, it was an ex Garda Police car, heck it still looked like it right down to the aerials on the roof and myself and my cousin were 2 tall dudes sitting in it. At the time President Bill Clinton had arrived in Ireland on a state visit and him and his convoy were traveling past Ennis to Galway as he was staying there in a Castle.

It was sheer coincidence, we were driving out of Ennis and suddenly from behind we saw the wave of Blue flashing lights and sirens, i pulled over to let it all past and then saw a gap in the convoy near the end, for the laugh i pulled into it totally expecting to be told off and then we heard another siren behind us. It was the rest of the convoy with a motor bike directly behind us and 2 more Garda cars.

I panicked and indicated to pull over but the motorbike Garda was waving at us giving the signal to speed up, suddenly we released that he thought we were in the convoy. So we kept driving and now we were part of the presidential convoy! It was surreal, so surreal. The turn came for the bar i was Djing in Galway but by now we were afraid to take it, we were going through red lights in Galway city now and panic set it, we were thinking what happens when we get to the castle? It was getting closer and closer and we suddenly saw our chance at the entrance. If you look back at the news coverage of the convoy entering the Castle you'll see all going in except for one lone blue Ford Mondeo that doesn't and instead drives past it from the convoy. That's us!

The job on the Station in Clare was great, I was given a chance by two people who ran it at the time and I felt hope, something I hadn't felt in a long time.

I was finishing my show and I took a call from a hotel manger called Martin. Martin was running a lovely hotel in Clare and wanted me to DJ in the Club the following week. That was the call changed everything.

I arrived to the gig in this pretty town and there was a lot of buzz that I was Djing there. I was brought in to the club and stood in the Dj Box waiting for the other Dj to introduce me, and then I saw her....

You know those scenes in the movies when a guy sees a girl across the dance floor and everything slows down?

That's what happened. Without saying too much out of respect for that girl, she stood by me through everything before finally and understandably giving up. When things get bad, she was there. It's safe to say that she helped me get through all this and got me out the other side. I'm eternally grateful to her and her family.

6. Ireland's Most Wanted.

It was a cold day in September 2005 and I was sitting in the car listening to the radio as often i did. I felt lower than normal. The day before I had read big news stories about me "taking" 2 cars from Waterford and Wexford, the articles had pictures of the cars and a big picture of me with "Catch him if you can" as the headline. I knew it wasn't me who took those cars, I was in Donegal and I could prove that, but who would listen? By now I was getting the blame for every bizarre car theft and crime in the country and it was getting out of control. My mind was in a bad place, and rather than face up to it again went into a fantasy world to escape what was really going on. All I could think of was my Girlfriend and how much I missed here but was afraid to see her.

I drove and drove and drove with the theme song from Back to the Future playing over and over again...don't ask. I can't even remember what I was thinking.

It started to rain and it was now night, i'd been driving all day and was now in Mallow in Cork, i hadn't eaten and had just traveled the length of Ireland, suddenly a car in front of me flashed the lights at me. In Ireland and elsewhere it's a sign that there is a Police Checkpoint ahead, i was driving a car from a "test drive" and it would have been reported by now so i indicated and drove up a smaller road instead. 40 mins had now past and i didn't know where i was and it was now after 2 am. I was in trouble, a strange car in a remote area would have been reported and Gardai would have to be called. I eventually found a slightly bigger road and a sign saying the name of a town 20 km.

As per usual i did not have any plan of where i was going or staying and was "winging" it. In the distance is spotted a car coming towards me, by now the rain had started to ease to a drizzle and it was hard to see too far ahead. The closer the car got to me the realization stated to kick in that it was a Police Car. As i got closer i noticed it had stopped by now waiting for me, and that would have freaked anyone out. I turned up the car aircon to max and pointed to at my face, i sat up as high as i could in the seat and i drove up to them and slowed down to stop and rolled down my window beside the Garda drivers window..

Fantasy kicked in..

"Well lads" I said in an articulate voice, "What has ye fuckers up here this late" i said and started to laugh. There was a pause of about 2 seconds before they responded which felt like a lifetime. They both started to laugh "We were about to ask you the same thing" the passenger said. I said the most Irish name i could think of (I won't say it here for legal reasons) I told them i had just finished a shift in Anglesea Street. You see Anglesea Street was the big Garda Station in Cork which was about 40 mins away, the shift change at that time was at 2am so it all made sense. We all spoke for about 3 minutes, they were mentioning names of lads asking how they were and i was bluffing my way through it all, not once did i say i was a Garda. It was all implied and if they were given out Oscars that year i was a definite contender.

We all said goodnight and eventually drove off.

Now, how else would you react if that was you? After i saw the car safely in the distance i screamed! A loud, deafening top of your lungs for 5 seconds scream. I could not believe that i had done what i had done. So now filled with adrenaline I drove and drove and drove. 3 hours later i had forgotten about it, but the Gardai it would seem had not..

7. Too many Close calls

It was a sunny Sunday at the beach in Mayo. I can't say that life was good because it wasn't. Now and then for a few minutes i would find myself surrounded by normality and it was in those few moments i forgot what was going on. It was a pretty beach with one lane leading down to it and being Sunday it was busy. Gay Byrne was on the Radio on Lyric Fm (Ireland's Classical Music Station) and i would always stop what i was doing to listen to him. He had a warmth to him that made you feel so relaxed and the music he played was from the 1950's era. Not exactly a Dj style but i liked the simplicity of the music back then. It was filled with emotion and the lyrics were powerful. It relaxed me.

I was parked on the beach with everyone else when i noticed a Ford Focus drive past me, the driver looked at me in one of those uncomfortable stares of recognition. I noticed immediately and had my guard up, maybe i was being paranoid? No, i wasn't and a few minutes later it drove past me again whilst watching me. Something was wrong and i felt it, I watched the car and saw the driver take out his phone, he had stopped a distance away from me trying to look in-conspicuous but made a mistake. He was parked facing away from me and while on the phone put his hand up on the rear view mirror to angle it towards me. I was in trouble now.

I had to do something quick, so i started to slowly drive down the beach past everyone including him to head to the lane to get out. Now it was a long lane from the beach the main road so the pressure was on. As i drove up i noticed the Ford Focus come behind me, i was definitely in trouble. As i went up the lane i could see he had his right hand out the window and he was waving at the cars behind him to slow down, i noticed then it had no tax or insurance disc on the window, it was a Police Car. I rolled my windows down and listened, in the distance i could hear a Police Siren coming closer, i had to think quick!

Now i was sweating, i turned the Aircon up full again and directed it to my face, i phoned the biggest Police Station nearest to the one that was closest to me, i knew what i was doing now. The polite Garda answered and i told him i was an off duty Garda at ...... Beach and noticed a wanted man Frankie Shanley there and could he confirm same with the other local Garda Station, i said i tried to get thorough to it but no-one answered. He told me to hang on and i could hear him on the radio, i could hear him talk to the driver of the Garda car on it's way to me (the siren in the distance) but not the Focus behind me, his radio didn't seem to be working so i had a chance here. I could hear them giving a description of my car i was driving and saying an off duty member was at the scene giving info. "Yes" the Garda confirmed, he has been spotted by a Garda there and a unit was on the way to apprehend him in his VW Passat, i had one chance here so i went for it. "Can you inform them that i'm now in front of Frankie Shanley " i then said "he is in a Silver Ford Focus, i'm the one in the Passat, someone has fucked up the information" to which he relayed to the Patrol Car and "Rodger" came the reply. Just then i spotted the patrol car at the top of the lane with the blue lights, i started to flash my headlights in a repeated 1, 2 quick motion, as if for a second to make them think it was the strobe of a police headlight, i was still on the phone to the Station so could hear that the focus hadn't made contact in this time. I accelerated a bit to make distance between me and it and as I got to the Patrol car i sat up as high as I could and put my hand out the window pointing back at the Focus and then indicating for them to move out of my way...and they did.

I drove past them and shouted out the window "Block the lane, don't let him out, i'm going to turn" and drove past them, they then blocked the lane and i could see them jumping out of the Patrol Car in my rear view mirror and run towards the Focus, it gave me a few minutes to quickly get into the maze of small roads in the area and i was free while they sorted out the confusion.

I love chocolate, it's my escape when i'm down, and god knows I put-on the weight back in those days, I was eating bad as being in takeaways was too risky for me (I was paranoid). It was Monday now and I drove to a small shop for food, at this stage i was well out of the beach area and relaxed a bit. I went into the shop which was small enough with two aisles and went down to the biscuit section, i was looking for my favourites and at the same time looking over my shoulder every time someone would walk into the shop. The door opened and a young guy came in with a News Paper, his words were "Lads wait till ye see this" Some things like that, even though it's 15 years ago i can remember.

He started to read the article to who i assumed was his friend behind the counter "Roscommon man wanted as he fools Gardai in late night Checkpoint" he started to read the story and what was a simple 3 minute incident on that night in Cork had now evolved into a Hollywood Movie version on the papers. He read out my name and how i was wanted Nationwide and i felt myself cringe as i heard what was being said. They continued to read and laugh and i saw my escape, i picked up the phone pretending i was on it and started to talk normal, the phone was on the side of my face by them so they could not see me and so i continued the imaginary conversation and walked out the door and back to the car which was now mentioned on the paper. I left and a few hours later was in Donegal again.

For some reason i always ended up by the Atlantic, i refused to go inland and i think it was the sound of the ocean that was my medication. I can remember sitting on an empty beach numerous times at night and praying this would all end soon. I would often sit there for hours and just drift off in my thoughts looking at the stars and feeling the breeze from the Ocean. It was a very bizarre time for me and if i'm honest things were not registering with me as to what i was doing, i was in day by day survival mode.

The following morning i woke up to my picture on the front page of a Newspaper again with the headline "Catch him if you can" now i had enough, my girlfriend had called me crying and it was the most heartbreaking thing i heard in my life ever. That moment i decide it was going to end now! But how could i do it? Who would listen to me? It was then i came up with the brainwave to "Talk to Joe".

Big Mistake..

8. Liveline

"Joe's very concerned" I was told by the producer of Liveline. Those words put me so much at ease and I agreed to go on air. Now if you're from Ireland you know who Joe Duffy is. If not, he is a Radio Presenter on RTE Radio and he presents a show called Liveline. Now to be fair, Liveline is responsible for so many good things coming to light in Ireland. He allows people on Air every day to get something off their chest and today it was Frankie's turn.

I spoke to Joe for 10 minutes i'd say, i told him all about how low i was and how scared i was, i explained how i was off medication for so long now and my mind was going crazy. To be fair he was a gentleman, he was comforting and genuinely was listening to help me. A Garda Inspector then came on Air to say that "Things are not as bad as they seem for Frankie" and "he should hand himself up to Gardai and get it over with and move on with his life". This was huge for me, this gave me so much hope and i could feel the immense pressure i was under lifting as i listened to the Garda Inspector.

The conversation ended, i left the phone box and i went back to the car. Now i have to tell you about my good friend Mike Conway from Tralee. Now and then we would meet just to talk and have some drinks and he was another escape for me with all that was going on. He's a good Kerry guy and one of the funniest people you will ever meet, and mad have we had some adventures that i could write another 5 chapters on. He made me laugh in those dark times and i needed that. I sat in the car and Mike was with me, he was laughing, he had the car radio on as i was On-Air and heard it all. Thankfully he's a good guy to be around in a crisis and he made a joke of it all even though i was embarrassed. I had met him many years ago on one of my many magical mystery journeys that even i didn't know where i was going, he joined me in Ballybunion in North Kerry many a time when i worked there.

I had met another good Kerry man by chance also, and through conversation it emerged he had just bought a hotel in North Kerry, we spoke over lunch and that day he offered me a Job. I spent many a good year in Ballybunion and met good people, looking back at those hotel days i miss them and him dearly. He had also seen good in me and done everything in his power to help me, he flew me around the Europe with his Big Dance show and he made me feel always like i had a purpose in life.

What a great man he was..

Mike Conway continued to make a joke out of the Phone-in and he had made me relax in doing so, we were joking away when suddenly I heard my name again being mentioned on Liveline, this time it was in anger. A Car dealer had phoned Joe to complain that he had given a "crook" airtime, he tore into me On-Air and accused me of taking a car belonging to him, well, to be fair I did.

He ranted on for 5 minutes and said

what the Gardai had said to him about me. Suddenly Joe Duffy said let's go to Cork now, and another Car Dealer came on again giving out about me, but this time he was saying i had taken a car from his garage when i didn't! I knew i didn't, yet here he was on National Radio saying i did, and then another came on and another and another and now it was just about me. It was crazy, the majority of callers who were saying i took their cars were wrong as i didn't. And out of the ones I did take no one was saying i had given them back a few days later. Joe was asking them the car values each time and by now it was all out of control. It was a free for all and anyone could now get on air saying what they wanted. I was shocked yet Mike now had tears in his eyes laughing.

We drove to Coleraine in Northern Ireland and i wanted to go to Asda for Chocolate, i was getting distressed and needed it. Mike came in with me and was trying to make me laugh but i was in a bad way. He told me to relax and that no one knows me up here. Then to prove it he shouted in a packed ASDA "This is Frankie Shanley everyone" "Do you know him" No-one batted an eye, Mike had proved his point in the most unconventional way.

Mike went home that day as i wanted to be alone to gather my thoughts. I didn't sleep one bit that night, so many thoughts going through my head and i couldn't understand how people were allowed On Air to accuse me of things i did not do. Now to be fair Liveline has changed since then and that would not be allowed to happen today. That night i spoke to my girlfriend for hours and i made the decision that for her i was going to hand myself up. The following day my picture was in every paper and even had pictures of the cars that the day previously i had been accused of, it even had interviews with the callers and i knew I was not responsible for the majority of those crimes.

1:45PM came and Liveline was back On- Air and straight away again it was callers about me, I was accused of so many crimes by now it was beyond belief, Grandfather clocks from houses while the owners slept, Sit on Lawnmowers and car after car after car. Now again, to be fair I had committed some crimes but in those 2 days on Liveline and the 30-40 crimes i was blamed of publicly, 6 i had actually done (Which i'm utterly ashamed of still) People were now messaging me to say that they were trying to get on air to defend me but Liveline wasn't allowing them on. After 2 days of what can only be described as an hatchet job at 5 minutes to 3 (show ended at 3) they allowed a caller on to defend me, it was the Hotelier in North Kerry, he spoke well for me and told everyone that they have no idea of what's going on with Frankie and that i was utterly lost right now.

I text Liveline and told them "I would be in custody in an hour and I was going to tell the truth and clear my name" which was read out on air, i phoned my girlfriend to apologise for everything and i drove to Manorhamilton Garda Station which was the nearest one to me at the time.

It was time to get my life back.....I thought

9. The Interview

I drove up to the gate on the Garda Station in Manorhamilton, a pretty little town in North Leitrim surrounded by some stunning scenery. There was an automatic barrier there with an intercom and so i pressed it "Hi can i help you" was the reply on the intercom, i said i was a Garda, i can't remember the name i gave but it worked, the barrier opened and i drove into the back of the Garda Station and parked the Volkswagen Passat i had taken for a test drive a few days earlier next to the Garda cars. I got out and walked to the back of the station, i was wearing a blue jacket and trousers, from a distance i looked like a Garda, it wasn't that i was up to something it was a psychological trick in case someone recognised me in a shop, they would assume that they knew me from being a Garda and it seemed to work..in my head

As i walked to the back door it opened and a polite young Garda walked out, i thought it was for me but he held the door open for me as he walked out to the patrol car, completely oblivious as to who I was. I walked into the station and there were 3 Gardai there, they were friendly and said hello, i felt my eyes tear up which was noticeable by the reaction of them and I said "I'm Frankie Shanley, your looking for me".

"Who" was the reply, "Joe Duffy has been talking about me for the last 2 days" i said and instantly it clicked with them. I was now in Custody.

The Gardai in Ireland are a very professional organisation made up of decent men and women. I have to say that I was treated with the utmost respect there at all times.

After the custody record was filled out i was placed in a cell. It was the most peaceful experience of my life, all the stress and pressure was gone, it was my chance to admit to what i had done and finally move on with my life and be with my girlfriend. Some time later 2 detectives entered the cell and introduced themselves to me, they would be questioning me. 2 very tall likable men who put me at ease. One of the detectives i had met in the last few years when i was DJing in Tullamore, we spoke for some time as he was now Superintendent there. I bought him a drink and we have both talked as friends every time we met which was so strange for me after everything.

In the meantime my solicitor had arrived and we spoke for some time, he told me to say nothing and he was going to get a doctor for me as something wasn't right. I told him i wanted to tell my side and I did not care if it meant prison as it was the right thing to do and the only way to end it. The doctor arrived and after a quick chat my solicitor voiced concerns abut my current mental state. The Solicitor again told me "Say nothing" as the crimes were all circumstantial and the fact that I was accused to the country on national radio meant a prosecution was not going to work.

But all I could see was my girlfriend's face, I could hear her crying in my head from the phone call previous and i did not take his advice. I wasn't in a good frame of mind and I should have said nothing, but I was willing to do WHATEVER it took to see her and move on.

Speaking to Gardai before my interview it was clear to them i wanted to clear the air, in fact they mentioned that from the outset in my book of evidence from 2005. In conversation at the station it was suggested by some Gardai that if i cleared the air it would probably be 1 court case and the majority of the crimes would be taken into consideration by the judge, now this would not have mattered to me wether i'd done them or not but more importantly i'd see my girlfriend sooner.

And so against Solicitor and Doctors advice i spoke from 5pm- 3am in the interview room admitting to every thing that was put to me. As far as I was concerned it was going to be one court case, the crimes were U.T's (unauthorised takings) and the maximum sentence was 12 months.

During the interview my only requests were for tea with lots of Sugar and Chocolate biscuits which i was given every time. Again the Gardai as always and those 2 detectives could not have been nicer.

The following morning September 2005 i woke up and was brought to the local district court, their were photographers waiting and i was feeling optimistic as my life was starting to sort itself out.

However in the court i was charged only with the crime of the Passat i arrived with, this was not part of the agreement and now i was getting worried, i had admitted to around 50 crimes and splitting them up was the nightmare scenario but that's what was happening. I didn't look for bail and was remanded in Custody for a week.

At some stage shortly after (i can't remember the timeline) my solicitor came to me, he said that he had spoken to a barrister, Gardai had made numerous errors with me. The custody record was wrong and technically the statement was now invalid and i should not have been interviewed according to a doctor. He said not to worry, if i plead "Not Guilty" at court i would indeed be found "Not guilty" on each one. He also said we would arrange bail which would be not much of an issue with the doctors report and i relayed the same to my excited girlfriend that night.

I was going to see her soon..i thought.

10. Systematic Torture

Now at this stage i should warn you that the next 2 Chapters are tough tedious reading, rather than overwhelm you with every detail i've narrowed it down as best i can. Please remember that i have state documents backing all of it up.

The following morning i was woken up by a prison office and told to get dressed, it was still dark outside and i was confused as to what was going on. I got dressed and

was brought to a Prison Van, in later years the same sight would break me but this was my first experience. I was handcuffed and placed inside a space smaller than a phone box, i could hardly breathe and started to get nervous. I was told i was being brought to Thurles in Tipperary for court.

The journey was terrifying, i was expecting a family visit that day in Castlerea Prison and meet my solicitor to arrange the bail hearing and also due to see the doctor to get the medication for my depression, We went down dark roads, it was bumpy and i was starting to panic as it was hard to breathe from the high heat and smell of diesel fumes, i called out to the officer for to ask for cold air and no one replied, i called louder and nothing, i was alone in the back and the prison officers were separate in the front and couldn't hear me, my breathing got faster. the noise was loud from the heavy van bouncing on the old roads. I screamed at the top of lungs in panic and banged the door with my handcuffs, i had lost it, completely lost it, i was terrified. They eventually heard me and came back to me. They brought me outside the van (breaking procedure) but they were decent people and i was clearly distressed.

One of them ran over the road to a shop and bought me water and after reassuring words and no heat we started the journey again. I arrived at the court in Thurles and was met there by a Garda who charged me with another car again separate to everything meaning i was now in serious trouble.

It was supposed to be one case, now it was two, then another Gardai appeared from Mitchelstown and charged me with a third car. The judge remanded me in custody to Limerick Prison and i was brought there instead of back to Castlerea. Every time you come into a prison you are considered "Fresh" and it does not matter if you were there the day before or 20 times that month. Being "Fresh" means you have to apply for a phone card (takes days) and apply for visits (takes a week) and you will be sleeping on the floor with 4 others until they get you a bed.

That night i was brought to Limerick and processed and placed in a cell (luckily enough) with another prisoner. Unknowing to me the prisoner was in for Murder and was not in a good state of mind. He would not speak to me and was talking to himself, i was getting worried. Some time in the middle of the night i woke up, he was banging the door of the cell calling for an officer. One came and he asked to speak to an "ACO" who is someone higher up and who can make things happen a little quicker. The officer told him he wasn't going to see anyone at night and out of the blue the prisoner said and i quote " If you don't get an ACO here now i'm going to burn this cell to the ground with me and him in it' Jesus, i started to sweat and shake, was he serious? He got his lighter and started to light the posters on the wall on fire, now i had to say something so i started pleading with him not to do this to me, in some way i think he realized it was wrong but it was too late, the door opened and 3 or 4 officers rushed into the cell and grabbed him, the bed was shaking (i was in the top bunk) and everyone was screaming. Eventually they got him out to protect me and the door closed. That was my welcome to Limerick Prison.

I got some sleep and was woken up again and brought to get dressed, i was told i was now going to Mitchelstown court, again the solicitor in Thurles had arranged to meet me in limerick that day to talk about bail and now i was going to miss him also. I was put in another Prison Wagon and brought to Mitchelstown, i had another panic attack in the wagon but the journey wasn't as long as the previous day. I arrived in Mitchelstown court and was met by 2 Gardai, one was dealing with my case today and another who surprise surprise was charging me with another car from my statement, i now had 4 active cases and bail would be impossible.

The judge was a colorful character who was feared by Gardai and Solicitors as an extreme Judge who often put solicitors in Custody and more. My case was read out and the Judge Interjected,

"Ah this man was on Joe Duffy's show" Now in the world of TV this would be grounds for a dismissal but in Ireland the legal system has many flaws and is not as perfect as it should be. Halfway through my solicitor defending me he again interrupted "I'm giving him 22 months in prison to keep him busy" there was shock in the court as maximum sentence was 24 months and i had a good defense but he did not want to hear it. His final remark when i was leaving was "say hi to Joe Duffy".

I was now in a bad way, this was only one of 50 sentences i was going to receive and it was 22 months alone! As you can imagine now the Newspapers had my picture everywhere almost every day. Every time i was brought to court and charged they would say i was at it again and make out like it was another crime i just committed, all the time they had no idea what was really going on. For the next 2 years i was in and out of court after court after court. This was the Garda's way to get around the statement and custody issue, spit them all up and force me to plead guilty.

If I pleaded not guilty to any of them i would have been found not guilty and cleared, but i would be stuck in the system in the meantime and prison for over a year per case before release, and at that stage i'd have gotten numerous other charges and the process would start all over again, and remember i had over 50 cases!

By now i had taken the advice of a nice Detective from Clonmel who knew i was in nightmare scenario, he said just plead guilty to everything on the first day to speed it up and end it, then appeal everything as one at the end, otherwise i would be in prison for years. This meant that now my Convictions were pilling up and every case was being treated as a new offence, so every time the sentences were getting more severe as it seemed like i wasn't learning my lesson and no News Paper or Court knew that in fact they were mostly connected to the one statement.

When i was brought to a court it was always by surprise, so as i said i had to plead guilty to avoid being brought back to that court 4-5 more times over the year, which meant i had no defense documents to show the Judge, the documents would have gotten me a suspended sentence when the judge read them but i would have to please not guilty and/or look for adjournments which i didn't want. Adjournments meant more movements and less phone calls home, and so the sentences came and were getting bigger as was my conviction count.

The way i was being charged seemed like it had some element of orchestration to it. It was on a drip feed basis. I would get to the end of one sentence and a few days before my release i would be charged with another crime from my statement and remanded back in Custody. I thought i had done the right thing in Manorhamilton and it was now being used against me. I wanted to hug my girlfriend so much and it was breaking my heart. I wasn't getting medication or many phone calls as i was being moved around from prison to prison to follow the judges and each case.

On a very small few occasions i didn't receive food the whole day as to save money the Prisons were holding me in various holding cells under courts waiting for a "pick up" from another prison that was there to take me with them. There were crossovers from prisons in those days that meant i missed food times. I was charged with the same offences in different parts of the country numerous times and the whole thing was a shambles.

My family could not visit me as they

did not know where i was, solicitors for my cases could not find me either meaning i only got to speak to the 3 minutes before every case, and because they were split up it meant almost 50 different solicitors. And so on it went. Now you do the math, i had 50 plus cases i had admitted to (remember i had committed less around 5-7 of them) and again if you plead not guilty you have to wait 1 -2 years in prison for your case and you still have 49 more to go. Can you imagine what was going through my mind?

In one case a few days before my first release i was brought to a court in Cahirciveen in Kerry, all i could remember was in 2005 i said i stayed in a Holiday Home for a night and didn't pay, i decided i would fight this one as a test as it was minor, yet when i arrived at the court i was charged with 5 counts of Burglary, they were using me to clean up the books, i was accused of entering houses in the area and stealing jewellery from homes while people slept upstairs. I was shocked, of course it wasn't me! I panicked over this and my solicitor done a panicked deal that i would plead guilty to 2 if they dropped the other 3 and they did, i was disgusted, it was a dirty trick. And sadly this happens a lot in some Irish Courts, you're charged with more than you commit sometimes and deals are done between your solicitor and the Garda as to what you will plead guilty to and what gets thrown out.

The attitude by some Solicitors is "It will all be ran in" meaning you serve the multiple offenses at the one time, so taking 1 or 2 extra didn't matter. In court the judge knew something didn't add up and wanted to know why the state were dismissing 3 serious charges of burglary? He didn't believe the reply the Gardai gave him and stated "something's not right here, but i can't put my finger on it" he then heavily sentenced me for what was initially going to be a minor thing.

Later in 2019 i met that same Judge in Killarney at a coffee shop by chance when i was Djing there, I introduced myself to him and we sat taking for a long time about life and he was delighted as he said he rarely hears a "good story" from someone he sentenced. I could have told him what had happened in his court that day but I saw how passionate he was about him work. He was proud of his career and what he stood for so I kept it to myself.

By now i had met with a solicitor from Carrick on Shannon who was a wonderful man, some prison officers were fantastic they knew i was in serious trouble and not allowed basic things like calls or visits, some officers would sneak me phone calls now and then, one was to that solicitor. He eventually met me and agreed to help me get to the High Court, i had numerous "habeas Corpus" entered to the high court to get me out and intervene and was never brought to them as i was "lost in the system"

The Solicitor contacted an independent Psychologist in the Prison and he was to prepare a file for my Bail Hearing. We spoke for a few hours which gave me hope as it was a Bank Holiday Monday so he was clearly taking me serious. The man was genuinely concerned about what was going on and he made a report.

A few days later in Cloverhill Prison i was asked to attend a meeting room for to talk to someone. When i got there he introduced himself as Prof HK (I'm using initials intentionally) and he was there to make a report for the state in response to the one i had gotten a few days earlier.

I did not like the man from the start, he

was very condescending and all he wanted to talk about was what he had heard on Liveline, he asked me how i done those crimes and was quoting the callers! He wasn't one bit interested in hearing about my hospitalisations growing up or my issues since making the statement and when i told him i didn't commit 90% of those crimes he laughed at me, i ended the meeting and walked out and hoped i would never see him again, but little did i know he would partly be responsible for my biggest sentence to come.

Eventually the day came when i was brought to the High Court.

Now make no mistake, this was huge task, i still had 30-40 cases in the system, some sentenced and some pending and others also with another 10 or so to come, there was no end to it.

I was brought to the cell in Cloverhill on Monday Morning for my High Court hearing. My Parents were there and it was my first time to be heard finally.

I was taken from the holding cell and brought to the dock, i saw my parents and noticed all the reporters and so many Gardai. I was called to give evidence and i spoke honestly about what i was going though, i told the judge 2 years ago i had handed myself up to do the right thing and now i was stuck in the system with no way out and scared. Then it was the Gardai's turn, they quoted Joe Duffy and the Newspapers which were printing the OTT and fake stories, and then they called their 2 witnesses. My heart sank, i remembered them, it was the 2 Gardai from Munster back when i was going thought the checkpoint at night. They got into the box and told the story of what happened.

I thought i was in serious trouble, they started to tell the story and i heard people start to laugh in the court, and then i saw the judge smile, it threw the Garda who was giving evidence, the Garda then said there are 9 more Garda Witnesses to come who traveled from all over Ireland. They then said that i have 11 days of a sentence to serve in Northern Ireland from another case connected to these from 2005 and that i should be kept in Custody (those few days are still going through the legal process to this day). The Judge interrupted them and said there was no need for more witnesses:

He said that he had "read all the reports and seen lots of evidence" of my Prison movements and my statement. He then said that he was "frankly shocked" by what he read and his exact words were "as far as i'm concerned it is Systematic Torture by the Irish state"

Systematic Torture!

There was a gasp in the courtroom and the Prison officer beside me gave me a gentle nudge with his elbow for support. He said he was consolidating every case into one for bail purposes and was granting me immediate bail. He then said that he was concerned to see " The might of an Garda Siochana from around the country in the Courtroom today to prevent my getting bail"

I thanked him and was brought back down to the cell with so much relief. i still had a long way to go but now people would read in the papers what's really going on and the Judges words. However of all the reporters that were there that day from all the reporters not 1 mention of that important hearing appeared in ANY paper meaning the true story was again hidden and so my fake persona continued in the media.

11. A New Hope

For a few weeks life was kinda normal, I was now living with my girlfriend and going to the cases still, but they had all been adjourned as per the high courts allowing me to get treatment for depression after my ordeal.

I received a call after a few weeks that my appeal for the sentence i had received in Mitchelstown Cork (22 months) was up in a few days. When the Garda called me i explained the story with the High Court and that i could get a letter from my Doctors with an update. He gave me the date and i went to the court sitting in Mallow. He said if I didn't go I would be arrested.

My Solicitor told me not to worry as the High Court ruling was in my favour. The case was called and immediately the State Solicitor went for it. He told the Judge i was a "Known Fraudster" who was on Joe Duffy and had fooled Gardai in the past, he was very aggressive and he did not mention the High Court. Then my Solicitor stood up he told my story but each time the state solicitor would interrupt with another dramatic statement. The judge asked abut the High Court and my solicitor waffled something that didn't make sense even to me, he was clearly flustered and didn't do his homework, he hadn't ANY high court papers!

The Judge sentenced me to 8 months there and then meaning all the work for the High Court was now finished as there was a new custodial warrant to over-ride everything . To say i was upset was an understatement, my girlfriend and i had gotten a new place to live and had hope now, no-one was excepting this to happen. I was put into the cell and taken to Prison again a broken man.

I went to Cork Prison that night and had

accepted my fate now. The following morning i was woken up early and handcuffed and dressed and brought to a court in Athy where i was charged with another car from my statement and remanded in custody. I was now stuck in the system again. For the next 4 days i was dragged from court to court and given more new charges. Hope was now gone. Little did i know that my Carrick Solicitor was behind the scenes arranging me to be brought back to the hight court. I arrived at the High Court again and thankfully the Judge remembered me and granted bail after the 8 months was up (a few days away) He also said that every time i would appear before him it would be a "quick procedure" and that he "was noting every time Mr Shanley had to come before him" for other courses of action (clearly a threat to the State).

This still wasn't appearing in any papers as bad news sells more than good.

Again, I felt hope, I thought I was going to see my girlfriend that night. Sadly after the case instead of being brought back to Cloverhill Prison Dublin to be released i was handcuffed and put on a Prison Wagon and brought to Cork Prison, i was now arguing with the Prison Officers which i never done, i just had to sign my bail and be released but they didn't want to know. I was now in the Wagon on the long journey to Cork prison and again broken. Jesus, writing this now i can feel all the absolute emotions and dread coming back to me.

That night was the night i tried to end my life in Prison, i had enough. I was done.

I was placed in a padded cell for 3 days for my own protection and i saw the humanity of the good Prison Officers and the Governor of Cork Prison who done everything to try and help me

including getting me "outside help"
from a psychologist who would get me
back on track and focus me again. It
was a very tough time as i had totally
given up, i didn't want to call anyone, i
was medicated a lot and sleeping, and if
i'm honest i'm glad i don't remember
any of those dark days.

I still have nightmares about that day
and when I go to bed (to this day) I have
to have the TV on in the background so
my thoughts don't drift and take me
back to those dark days.

I was brought to Court in Munster and it
was the same Judge from Mitchelstown
and the 2 Gardai from the
checkpoint..yet again. I was charged
with THEFT of a car from Newmarket
in Cork.

Now this was odd because every single
car case before was a charge of
"U.T" (which is when you take a car but
give it back, for example if you took

your dad's car and were stopped by police) the maximum extreme sentence is 12 months whereas the maximum sentence for theft is 10 years, so why was this different and why were those 2 Gardai there again?

Now let's be clear about this as this case is very important, this is one of those many cars i did not take, remember that for later. The judge oddly granted me bail after hearing about the high Court meaning my bail was safe.

After the 4 months i was released and now had adjourned all my cases again so i would have some freedom. I arrived home that day a relaxed man and had tea with my parents. My parents lived in the centre of Boyle on a street where everyone knew everyone, it was nice. A knock came to the door, a loud knock, we all looked at each other and dad sent out, it was a Garda. He said he wanted to speak to me and so i went out, he handed me a sheet of paper with a number on it and said to call it which i did. It was a Garda from Tipperary, i called him and he said he had a charge for me for a car from my statement in 2005, i asked him why he was leaving it until hours after i was just released from Prison and years later but he would not answer me.

He said to bring a lot of money IF i was to be granted bail.

IF....

Now i'm sure by this stage you're getting fed up reading about these cases, now imagine me and my emotions, the constant high of getting out and the instant fall of prison again. And again, whilst the Gardai were only doing their jobs something was wrong.

That day, i gave up and i packed my bags and went on the run, i ran for 2 years constantly looking over my shoulder and becoming a recluse and i drank to forget.

12. TV3 and T.B

In February 2011 i was finally arrested and put back into custody. By now some time had passed and i was ready for what was ahead of me. Something had changed this time and i don't know what, i was put in Cork Prison and was being brought to my cases and returned there every night. This was different, my calls were now regular as were visits and it seemed, well, easier. One of my first cases to get out of the way was in Clifden in Galway. I arrived at the court after the long journey and to my horror saw it was the Judge i was on "Protection Duty" with at the start of this book. It was awkward. We were both awkward. I kept my head down and said nothing. The Prison officers afterwards asked me "what was that about, do ye know each other" I told them and they laughed, heck i laughed then.

I was brought one day to Cloverhill prison where i was given 3 more charges from 2005, two were for cars and one for a Video Camera. I was placed in Cloverhill Prison (Dublin didn't count for same day back to Cork) but it was okay, the Governor in Cork was a good man and he had done something to ensure i was kept in Cork. In Cloverhill i was placed on C1 landing which is where people that are not dangerous are placed. Again, good friendly prison officers that had a horrible job but knew you were different and would help you. I was put in a cell with 3 Malaysian guys and i slept on the floor for a few days.

During that time i noticed one of the guys above me was very sick and coughing a lot, he had a strange mark on his arm and there was blood regularly on his tissues. The other prisoners were afraid to go near him and now me, the rumours were it was TB. It was surreal few days as there were posters warning prisoners about how not to catch TB (which they always denied was there) but it didn't matter as shortly after i was moved back to Cork. As i said i was working in the Kitchen there and time was going quickly as i now had structure after all those years.

One morning a Prison officer came in looking for me, now this was strange as it was after 10am so it was not Court, i was cuffed and brought to the Chest Clinic in Cork. I had no idea what was going on, i went in and saw a Nurse who told me there was an outbreak of TB in Cloverhill and contact tracing lead them to me as i was in the cell with the person. She said it was just procedure and i should be fine. She gave me the first test and told me they would send me the results in a few days. However the following morning i was again brought back to the clinic but this time she seemed concerned, my first test had come back as Positive for TB. This was serious, but she needed to be sure and so another test was given to me, it was a strange kind of needle injected above my hand and i again was sent on my way.

That night i started to feel unwell, i was sweating a lot and had a head ache. My cell mate Brendan was a lovely guy from Midleton in Cork and a gentleman, he was in for something small. He made me tea and was so good to me, as he was handing me the tea he asked me what wrong with my hand, i looked and it was starting to swell badly were i had gotten the needle earlier. It was the same mark i had seen on the Malaysian guy in Cloverhill Prison. A day or two later i was brought back to the hospital and a shocked Nurse told me it looked like i had TB as my reaction from the needle was in line with someone positive for it, she took blood test and took note of my being unwell.

Through all this i was still dealing with courts and all the drama surrounding them including the daily news articles. Soon after i was brought back to Hospital and told that i was confirmed as having TB, jesus, on top of everything else now i had this to deal with! I was told that it was latent but there was a real concern that i was starting to get sick. Because of this a referral was made to see a specialist in October and the Prison and Public health would be notified immediately. I returned to the Prison and was placed back at work in the Kitchen, this was worrying after my diagnoses and when i mentioned it to the Prison doctor i was laughed at (happened a lot) and told " You don't have TB"!

Yes you read that right!! I was returned to Work in the kitchen but now was more worried than ever. Rumours started circulating that i had TB and some prisoners were avoiding me and refusing to take food off me.

Night times were relatively calm in Prison in Cork, Brendan was a good lad and we had great chats. One night we were both drinking tea and relaxing and put on a New Show that has started on TV3 Called "Beware Ireland" it was about Dodgy Car dealers and took our minds of things. At the end of the show it gave preview of what was on next week and it was called "Conmen" and to my shock it had a picture of me! Suddenly there were cheers in the prison of "Go on Frankie" and more.

I didn't need this, i was trying to keep a low profile and had cases still pending, by now i had almost 65 convictions. My heart sank from shame.

The next day was weird in the Prison, people were looking at me and in prison that's a no no. I did my job and again was refused the medication for TB when i went looking for it as they kept saying i didn't have TB (I have documents stating same).

6:45pm i arrived back in the cell after talking to my girlfriend. I entered the cell and was talking to Brendan, i had my back to the door, we were talking about something simple when all of a sudden i felt a big bang to the side of my head, it was something hard and solid and i dropped to the floor, the ringing noise was deafening in my ears and i couldn't open my eyes,

when i did it was blurred and then i saw red and then nothing......

I woke up in Cork University Hospital, i didn't know what was going on, i was in a wheelchair and i couldn't see, i asked what was going on and i was told i was knocked unconscious from behind by another Prisoner with what they thought was a steel bar. He was annoyed that i had served him food when i had TB. I could feel blood dripping down my face but i couldn't open my eyes, after some time in the hospital i felt someone put a surgical mask around my mouth, i could hear the nurse giving out to the officers, she was saying "He has TB and should have a mask on at all times until the specialist sees him". So i sat there, bandages around my head covering my eyes, surgical mask around my face, handcuffed and in a wheelchair.. Jesus.

I received stitches that night but was unconscious most of the time, when i eventually woke up i was back in my cell. The following day i was brought to court in Ennis for a case, i was in bits, to add insult to injury on the journey there i was again handcuffed in the wagon and who was cuffed in the box next to me? The guy who had assaulted me, he was subtly threatening me that he would get me if i pressed charges and that prison was small place and i was known. It really wasn't worth the hassle.

In Ennis court to my amazement a Probation offered to intervene and help me after my Solicitor suggested it, but the Tipperary Garda in the case stood up and told the Judge that "You can't do that Judge, he has hundreds of warrants outstanding around the country" the court room and the judge and me were all shocked, this was news to me, the judge asked for proof and the Gardai after

fumbling through papers for 2 minutes said he hadn't it to hand. The judge adjourned the case for two days to allow the judge to see the proof.

The following day a new headline appeared in nearly every News Paper in the land entitled "CONMAN WITH HUNDREDS OF WARRANTS TO BE

SENTENCED" this was shocking and false as i had none. That night the TV3 documentary again aired and my Persona was again sealed.

The day came for the court and the Garda stood up to the court and apologized to the Judge (not me) and said that he "had read Pulse (Garda Computer) wrong" and that "there were no warrants outstanding". My barrister stood up with all the newspaper clippings and tore into the Garda for doing what he had done to me to stop a Probation intervention, the Gardai then told the court "In relation to that, i spoke to probation this morning and they now want nothing to do with him".

The Judge's hands were tied, there was obviously some kind of intervention that made them change their minds. The Judge sentenced me and the headline the day after read "CONMAN SENTENCED" with no reference to the mistake the Garda made, meaning that up until 2019 that headline of "Conman with Hundreds of warrants" was still on Google with all the other stories and caused me untold damage. I was then brought back to Cork Prison with another big sentence from my statement in 2005. Now to be the fair the court reporter in Ennis where i was sentenced is a good man, i contacted him in 2018 voicing my concerns about the headline and he had it removed.

For the next few months i was between Cork Prison and Cloverhill Prison, by now i was getting medication in Cork but every time i was brought to Cloverhill it stopped, i was arguing daily to get them and as i've said before was regularly punished by staff as they were going by what Professor HK had told them (documents available). There were times i was placed in a cell with the worst of the worst as punishment to be kept quiet, this is backed up by FOI docs and Prison movement records. It was so frustrating. The TB medication was vital to me, i was warned NOT to stop taking it and keep it regular or it would damage my liver and more. But by now my bowels had stopped moving as the starting and stopping of the medication every time i came to Cloverhill was now having an effect. FOI documents from Castlerea show a letter the doctor sent to Roscommon hospital, he thought i had bowel cancer, i had a lump in my bowels, he was very concerned about me and ordered urgent tests, but the tests never happened as i was moved again to a different Prison. I now had a lump and was losing weight and in a very bad way. Through all this i was still being brought to court and getting sentenced without documents to defend myself as by now i didn't care, i had to end them, and so more articles appeared calling me a "Conman" with cases i hadn't committed and then came the TV show which by now was airing twice a week.

Let's talk about the "Documentary" featuring me. It was awful, it had a Radio man from Galway speaking to camera for ten minutes about Crimes he said i had committed using his name, now i have to point out that i was never questioned and never sentenced in relation to anything to do with him, as far as i'm concerned he was using me to publicise his radio show. I would have had loved to taken legal action against him but the costs upfront were huge. In Ireland, no money, no justice.

Then came the Vectra car from Newmarket in Cork, the garage owner was in studio talking about how i impersonated a Garda and asked for the car to be parked up and then took it. Then came a court reporter from Dublin who relished the chance to be on TV. Now remember i had NOT done this crime, but here i was on a Nation-wide TV Show being accused of all these crimes and quoting old articles from other cases i had not committed, no mention of the high court or any of the issues and everything making out that i was doing this for years and not stopping.

As I said this show was repeated every week for almost 2 years on both TV3's National stations and again caused my fake persona to get out there in the worst possible way. For the next few months i was arrested numerous times by Gardai in relation to other Liveline callers from back then who had now made statements because after seeing the documentary i was now hated. I was so disappointed that no one was printing the truth and everyone wanted to jump on the bandwagon. I have multiple documented evidence from Gardai stating "No charges will be brought re these incidents" as other people had been convicted.

It was there when i realized my only hope was to get out and prove people wrong.

Cases came and went and now i only had 1 left in Dublin.

The morning came for the last car and the video camera, i was sitting in the holding cell and was anxious but happy it was all finally over, The solicitor and the Garda had told me it wouldn't be bad and not to worry. It was a Camera & a U.T, and a few days previous i was given 1 day in prison for a U.T in Cavan by a good judge who saw the Psychologist's report defending me, and he saw through what the state were doing.

The case was called and i was listening to the Garda giving evidence and he was very fair, he wasn't dramatic and was very professional, he said i'd been through a lot over my statement in Manorhamilton and he was confident i had learned my lesson. Everything was calm and relaxed until the sentencing came. The Judge lifted up a thick file which she was given by Professor Harry Kennedy (HK) the state psychologist at Cloverhill.

He said i was a "Habitual Fraudster" who has never learned his lesson, he said i had been committing these crimes shortly after being sentenced for others since 2005 and it was clear i wasn't learning my lesson (wrong of course). He said i was bragging on Joe Duffy for 2 days where victims came on to tell how i had ripped them off (wrong again) he said that i was never in a hospital over depression growing up and never had it (wrong and documents prove that) he said i was using it all to get out of these proceedings.

He said he was confident that i would never learn my lesson and needed a big sentence as a deterrent. Then he said that even while in Prison i was trying to Scam the system by pretending to have TB to make money. The court was silenced, the Garda looked at me with a look of confusion. No one had seen this coming and i was blindsided by that horrible man.

FOI Documents received a few years ago show that Professor HK told Cloverhill prison to stop my tablets for depression as i was making it up and that's why i wasn't getting them when i should have. He also told them to STOP ALL MEDS! That's why i wasn't getting the TB medication in Cloverhill, i had even been punished numerous times in Cloverhill for saying i had TB and now it all made sense.

The FOI Documents from the Prison Computer are shocking. (In 2019 the state brought me back to Ireland and gave me a very quiet settlement for getting TB in prison and all that occurred but that didn't appear in any newspaper despite my sending the media all the documents for balance on the bad stories)

That day, that judge over a fake report sentenced me to 7 years in prison with 4 suspended.

The newspapers printed another big headline story which again did not have the real story and it added to the fake news already out there and my Persona. One even had a full page saying "CONMAN TO SUE THE STATE" and it implied i was now on top of everything pretending to have TB to get out of prison and get money.

A few days later i was called back to Cork for the Newmarket car sentencing, remember the one? The TV documentary which aired for 2 years? Now this case is important as it was a "test case" for me, i pleaded not guilty and opted for a trial. I needed to send out a message to everyone what was going on and this was my chance.

The Garda came into the cell to say hi, a lovely man, he asked how was i holding up as it was clear to everyone now what was going on. I told him i was struggling and his words to me that morning in the cell were "Don't you worry about this one lad, everything will be okay"

To my surprise the state withdrew the charge in Court as someone else was got for the crime. My solicitor wrote to TV3 and suddenly the documentary vanished and has not been seen since..anywhere, even on youtube...gone!

After being aired nationwide weekly at 9pm for over a year accusing me of it and disgracing me..Shocking!

Thankfully we are at then end of my sentences...almost.

I was moved to Castlerea in Roscommon which was the release i needed. It was a series of houses in a closed prison to get you ready for release. Staff were good and there was a hint of normality.

3 Months before my release in early 2014 i was given yet another charge relating to my 2005 statement, now this time it was different, the judge saw through it all and when asked "why now" the state said that it "got lost in the system" The Judge did not agree and suspended my sentence.

The day i was told i was leaving prison i remember to this day, it was all finally over, there was nothing else out there, it was over and i was going home.

Now i had to clear my name and tell the real story.

13. They think its all over..

The day i finally got out of Prison with no more cases was a major relief for me, except i didn't feel as excited as i should have been, i think that because i'd had so many bad things happen in the past when something good happened, i was now immune to any emotion. I met my girlfriend and i started the process of rebuilding my life and clearing my name. It was tough, there were many setbacks but i fought hard.

All i could do was Dj yet no-one would hire me, everyone was believing what was in the Papers and on TV over the years and i was now untouchable. When i did contact venues i would get a nasty reply. By now i was getting abuse and was the joke of other Dj's who knew i was back and trying to get into the business. Now and then someone would give me a gig and i would fill the venue for them night after night, but then i would get the dreaded "Were okay for now" message and i would then be blocked.

Eventually the hotelier in Ballybunion gave me my break again when no one else would and i was thrust back into a job almost 2 months after release in the hotel. It was very hard, i went back on Social Media and started to post that i was back DJing. Then the messages started to come into the Hotel. What people didn't realise was that i was also in charge of Social Media for the hotel at the time so saw every message.

It was a DJ from Limerick (well known) telling them about my past and warning them to stay away from me as i would "steal all their equipment". Now there were "reports" in papers back in the day saying i was doing this, but again , i wasn't and never did. I was also never questioned in relation to anything like that. I was quite shocked that this Dj would go out of his way to do this but then more shocked when i read the rest in which he said he would DJ at half price for them instead of me to "help". (This happened to me at least 20 times in the next 4 years and as recently as last year 2019 in Westport)

I kept going and took fall after fall after

fall, and always in the same circumstances of another Dj messaging the venue, by now i was an easy target for this as Google would back up what the Dj was saying and still had the most awful headlines including "CONMAN WITH HUNDREDS OF WARRANTS TO BE SENTENCED" but again, what was really going on wasn't printed anywhere. Now at this stage i had developed a drive to success which sadly took me over. I kept going, i would regularly sleep in train stations after a gig as i couldn't afford a hotel after paying big money travelling. For me i didn't care, every gig was my clawing my reputation back step by step so it was worth it and especially in Kerry things took off for me.

I was now Djing in upmarket hotels in Limerick and things were taking shape. In early 2015 i decided i was going to try and get back to Radio, it was going to be hard with all the extreme publicity but i was determined to do it.

So in Feb 2015 i decided to create my own radio station. I spent many a sleepless night doing it all myself, website, apps, logos, jingles and more importantly the music, i had developed a knack of finding New Music before anyone else and so that was the focus of the station. It was a mammoth task but in April 2015 Z1 launched. Now straight away it took off, artists were tweeting about it playing their song first and the listenership figures were over 30k which for a new online station was huge, month after month the figures rose and rose and at one stage over 100k were listening from around the World. Then it went stateside in the USA, i linked up with a major Hip Hop artist (Dj Infamous) and he broadcast a show live from the states 4 times a week after my show, and then came Greece. I was offered a Summer residency on a Greek Island and i jumped at the chance, it was huge!

Radio wise it was a major thing, in May 2015 Dj infamous was live from the USA and handed over to me live from a beach on a Greek island! It was so cool, the sound quality was as good if not better that the national stations and the figures went through the roof.

It was then that a well known Global microphone company came to sponsor it, that made a huge difference because now a Global Sponsor was on board. Then we had a show live from Australia after me, it was piggy backing all over the world and the technology involved was a lot of work yet all done by me. Suddenly i was getting messages from Zane Lowe from Apple's Beats1 Station (which launched a few months after my station) congratulating me on Z1 and my success, now this again was a major thing and it was the boost i needed and so i contacted Irish Newspapers and the Radio Website over there but sadly no one would write a piece about it.

Again my story was not being told and only the bad news was still there on Google to damage me. Zane Lowe has given me so much advice in the last few years and has helped me a lot when i asked him for it.

In the 352 days of 2016 i done around 300 Dj gigs (7 night residency in Greece). I was determined now to prove to everyone that i was working hard, but still no one knew and assumed the worst. I was getting messages of "Cop yourself on, no one believes you" and much worse every time i would post on social media my Djing in Greece.

Now one thing that has remained the same from day 1 is that people can be nasty, and if there is one thing worse than someone doing good for themselves in Ireland it's someone doing well that shouldn't be, and so jealousy always creeped in and it was relentless.

How dare i be doing well! The abuse started, i was getting messages saying i should be ashamed of myself, one said i should kill myself as i'm an embarrassment, another hoped i would die painfully of cancer, others instead of contacting me would contact my advertisers or places i was Djing in and they would inevitably pull out and sack me. They were horrible and in the last 6 years i have made at least 8 complaints to Gardai but sadly nothing ever happened about it.

Now and then a fake Twitter account would appear with links to the old News Stories and they would tag any artist or company involved with Z1 saying it was all a con. I can't begin to tell you the amount of money this cost me from advertisers pulling out and it was impossible to deal with.

For years i have contacted Google with proof of the stories that are false and every year they have moved the goal posts for me and so i've given up asking them now. I'm not going to win, bad news gets clicks and it's as simple as that. 15 years later those bad stories are still on Google damaging me and will be for the rest of my life. One of the most upsetting things is making so many good friends and getting good jobs and then losing every single one of them all over these Google listings.

All i could do was be successful and over power the bad listings with eventual good ones. So i started to fight back more and harder, now i was sleeping about an hour or two a day as my mind was on overload with ideas and that was good as now i couldn't have the nightmares that i was having.

It was a horrible situation, i only had Facebook and Twitter to use to show the World what i was doing but it was leaving me open for abuse.

I then started to drink way too much to help me forget what was going on in my life and that backfired. I was making friends who the day after would ignore me and suddenly develop an extreme hatred to me. Google gave them the impression i was up to something and i eventually gave in to it and resigned to the fact i wasn't going to make any more friends.

To this day i'm afraid to get too close to anyone for fear of the inevitable fallout.

14. A Lack of Intelligence

What happened next is a big part of this book, in fact it's one of the main reasons i wrote this. Later on the Gardai and GSOC (Garda Ombudsman) will officially say that this never happed because of an investigation by a Garda Superintendent , yet 3 years later in November 2019 they will back track and say that it probably did. The next few chapters are hard reading but everything is backed up by FOI documents from the Irish State.

In early 2017 i came back to Tralee, by now Z1 was a major station and well known. This is when everything changed for me, I think it was January when i was approached by an investor who wanted to take Z1 to the next level, now this was it! This was what i was waiting for, the excitement was too much, it was big money and so i decided to turn Z1 into a business. The deal was i would get the money on a certain date after i had fulfilled all i was asked (which made sense) to make Z1 a business. I rented a beautiful Studio space in Kerry and bought some proper Studio equipment, i then got a B&B in

Tralee and started to build Z1 up. Through all of this i was regularly meeting my investor and always at the same place in the Grand hotel in Tralee. He was as excited as i was and we had a plan to take Z1 to FM.

It was a beautiful Wednesday in Tralee, i stood outside the Grand Hotel Tralee waiting for my investor and life seemed to be taking shape for me, i was still travelling the country doing gigs for little money but i now had a plan. As i was waiting i noticed a Garda car come around the corner at the AIB bank, this happens of course but this was odd, it was driving slow and they were looking at me as they went past, something didn't seem right. I waited and waited and waited, no sign of my investor, normally i would meet him outside at our agreed time but this was strange, i then rang him and he wasn't answering which wasn't normal for him. I eventually gave up and went back to the

Studio to do my Breaking Music show which was me playing New Music First, days ahead of most stations around the world and the Irish Radio Stations. The show ended and still no word from my investor. Maybe he's sick, i thought?

By now i was also DJing regular in Killarney as well as Tralee and was keeping busy, these two venues knew about my problems and it felt great to be excepted and not have to worry about losing the gigs. So i decided to rent a house in Killarney for myself and booked it and checked in. I was there a few hours when i finally received a call from my Investor, he seemed different, he said that he now wanted nothing to do with me or the station. I was gobsmacked, not only did we have an agreement but i was after getting the Studio and all this expensive equipment. I pushed him to know why but he hung up.

I cried that night, why me, why, why,

why! I was letting my partner down again! I texted my investor and i can't remember what i said but it was from the heart and not angry. It must have resonated with him because a few minutes later he called me back. Now this call and what he told me would change my life for the next 3 years and cause me so much stress and heartache all over again. He told me that a Garda had called him warning him about me, the Garda said that i was under surveillance and that i was bad news, he apologised to me but said it wasn't worth the hassle of it all and he hung up..

Please, read that again...

I didn't know what to do, so many thoughts were running through my head and needless to say i did not sleep that night.

It was around 2pm and i was at home trying to make sense of what was going on, the hardest part was that i was missing my partner so much, but i had this drive to show people that what they read about wasn't true and that was what i was focusing on. it was now taking over my life.

I was drinking a cup of coffee and relaxing in my house in Killarney when i heard some drama in the driveway. The door knocked and there was my landlady, her husband and their father, they weren't happy, they gave me 15 mins to pack and get out of their house, i was speechless and confused, they said they knew EXACTLY who i was and they wanted me out now. By now my emotions had kicked in, it wasn't anger, it was sadness and i was visibly upset so i and asked them why?

Now they are good people because the husband obviously felt sorry for me and he told me that a Garda called "Frank" from North Kerry had telephoned them warning them to get me out as i was bad news. I didn't know what to say but i packed my bags and offered to pay them for that week as i left, to be fair they would not accept it, they just wanted me gone. And so on a that day in Killarney i walked the 2km to the train station with my arms full of my stuff and my tail between my legs. I walked to the station (the father to be fair had stopped asking if i wanted a lift but i was too ashamed over what happened to accept) i phoned the B&B in Tralee that i normally stayed in and they seemed off also. I was told there was no room for me and they were full. It didn't seem right, so after a while i phoned again with a different voice and i was told there was a room.

Something awful was going on, and i had again lost everything.

In the following days i had no choice but to return the Studio equipment and was told to leave the Studio i had gotten, i was in serious financial difficulty now and ended up getting a "loan" from a good friend to pay back my huge debts which i was paying back until 2019. I struggled, my partner was paying bills alone and i couldn't help as i was paying my debt from the collapse of the station. They were awful times. There was one venue in particular that was good to me, the Abbey in Tralee which is owned by the Leane Family, a wonderful bunch of people who i just adore. They were a massive help and put me back DJing to take my mind of things.

It was now around Feb 2017 and it was my first night Djing in the Abbey in a long time, it was the night of a big Soccer match, i can't remember, i think it was Ireland and France or something like that. I started the gig after the match and i felt my worries escape albeit for a few minutes, i looked up and noticed 2 Gardai in full uniform inside the door standing looking at me in front of everyone, i put my head down and continued, one of them was the Garda i saw drive past from the day at the Grand hotel Tralee.

15. The Wrong Man

I was sitting in the Abbey with a drink, i always looked out of place, i was the popular Dj but was afraid to talk much to people. By now i was used to the rejections the day after and the inevitable hatred they would develop when they Googled me, so it was best to stay alone. Everyone in the Abbey knew by now but they were trying their best to make me feel welcome and i appreciated that. It was people like them that gave me hope in humanity and kept me going.

My phone rang at the bar, it was a

private number, normally i'd panic but my Pint made me think otherwise. I answered it and there was friendly voice asking me if i was Frankie the Dj, i told him i was and he said he wanted to book me for a party and i agreed, he asked me to come to a bar (he named it) which was on the Square in Tralee, and he would give me a deposit and i agreed, i mean, he sounded okay.

I walked out of the Abbey and turned right to go to the Square, now there are two ways into the Abbey, the first is the main double door at the car park and the second is the side door, i walked out the side door.

As i walked past the cafe almost at the square there is an alley way to the right that leads to the Car Park where you would come on if you left the double doors. I walked past it and heard a voice calling "Dj Dj" from that area.

I walked over and saw a man standing

under the tree that's in the corner (and looking back now he was out of CCTV range) He looked respectable but was nervous, he was looking around and told me to listen to what he had to say.

He told me he was a Garda from Tralee and that he and others were concerned over what was going on in the Station, he told me he knew how hard i was working and he wanted to show me something, he then showed me screenshots of page after page (over ten) of Garda Intelligence from the Pulse System. They were all under the heading NATIONWIDE FRAUDSTER ALERT and had all my movements from last few weeks, it had everyone i spoke to, where my house was in Killarney and the B&B and even my being outside the Grand Hotel in Tralee meeting my investor. It was serious and very detailed and all compiled by the same Garda. For now and to avoid confusion lets call him Garda X.

Suddenly everything made sense to me, my getting evicted, losing the investor, the B&B, gigs i had lost, and mysteriously they were all named here. The Good Garda told me the he was concerned as Garda X seemed to have an agenda to get me, he told me that there was Conman travelling the country at that time stealing from old people pretending to be a Garda and Garda X was insinuating it was me. He told me my picture had being circulated to every Garda station in Ireland and that a few nights ago Garda X was overheard in the station saying "lets go see Shanley" before coming into the Abbey Bar in full uniform to stare at me (remember earlier).

He then gave me what he called "Digital Breadcrumbs" that i was to give to GSOC

which would confirm beyond any doubt

that the information i was given was from an official Garda source and would direct them to the intelligence and that i then would not and could not be doubted. Other stuff was said that for legal reason i won't mention here for fear of revealing his identity. He then told me to wait a few weeks before i complained as it would deflect from his "Enquiries"on Pulse.

Now those few weeks were hard, i wanted to scream from the top of my lungs but i couldn't, i was utterly frustrated, i was used to getting abuse from people over Google but this was different, this was a Garda and he had cost me everything including my business. At this point my relationship started to go downhill, i was impossible to deal and live with and had no patience, i was taking it out on her and i was now on the verge of insanity. After a few weeks past i made an extremely detailed statement to GSOC about Garda X and i also went to Tullamore to make a Criminal Complaint of harassment against him. I had nothing, and no one would hire me now, i was losing work at a crazy rate and a gig i got in Cork came crashing down when i received a summons for being in that venue after hours. I was DJing there and staying there and was tidying up my equipment. It cost me over €1000 to defend and was eventually thrown out by the Judge in Bandon who took my side.

Around the same time i wanted to to the right thing and give something back, i offered to build a radio studio and online station remotely for my local college back home. The principal and i spoke for weeks and i went and spent what little money i had for the equipment for them. Out of the blue one morning he called me to tell me someone tipped him off about Google, his tone was nasty now and made me feel awful. He said he wanted nothing to do with me.

Here i was again trying to do the right thing and now i had more equipment i had to sell as i didn't need it now. The months i spent developing the station and website and apps, i just had to delete them all.

I was offered more work in Greece and gladly took it to get away, my plan was to eventually stay there.

I finalised all with GSOC who had now started the investigation and then moved abroad.

Greece is heaven, i adore it, but i was lost without herself and it was hard. Days turned to weeks and i kept watching my emails for an update on my Investigation, Eventually out of the blue i received an email from a Garda Superintendent. This shocked me, what did he want? He asked me to meet him to come back to Ireland and make another statement to him (my 4th one now) about Garda X but he wanted the name of the Garda who told me.

Now alarm bells were going off and i was then told that GSOC had PASSED my independent investigation to a GARDA Superintendent (him) to investigate! Now firstly i didn't ask for this and secondly he was 10 km away from Tralee where Garda X was, and everyone knew that that same Superintendent was due to move to Tralee to take it over, meaning Garda X would be acting under him in a few months. Something was seriously wrong now and again i was being shafted.

By now i had googled Garda X and realised what was going on, he was initially in Macroom in Cork and his Sergeant and Unit dealt with me in 2005, (he also worked with the Gardai from the late night Checkpoint) the Car in Newmarket that i was accused of (the focus of the documentary that disappeared after 2 years). The same car that someone else admitted to and the state threw out even though i was blamed for it on TV.

He had then been moved to Tralee and had seen me. He automatically assumed i was up to no good and started to compile the intelligence about me when he heard about the Conman traveling the country. I was now officially under Garda surveillance and my image was in every station in Ireland. I refused to come back to make another statement to him as i was working now under contract in Greece, i told him i had made multiple statements already and that i would talk to him in October. A few weeks later GSOC sent me an email to say that they were CLOSING the investigation on foot of directions from the Garda Superintendent who found NO INTELLIGENCE being compiled about me by Garda X.

He then said that i refused to co-operate and to meet him to make a statement and would not reveal the details of the Garda who gave him the information. Just think about that. FOI later will show he also sent GSOC my list of previous convictions to discredit me (independent investigation remember). He told them he was concerned his officer would have to wait months for me to come back and it would cause him considerable stress which wasn't fair on him.

I was raging, now i was angry as i knew that was a lie. A Garda Superintendent was now misleading and impeding a GSOC investigation to protect his officer. I wrote to GSOC for an appeal and they refused saying the the Superintendent had done a very thorough investigation and found no intelligence. It also said i refused to give him the name of the Whistleblower.

In all my dealings with GSOC since this i was treated with utter contempt, they were awful to me and made me feel stupid and constantly agreed with the Gardai. I wasn't believed by them now, they sided with the Superintendent that i was making it all up and had a "gripe" with Gardai.

Last year i received hundreds of Freedom of Information Documents from GSOC which show that not only did the Garda Superintendent lie (no other word for it) but they also show that my Criminal Complaint against Garda X was sent from Tullamore to Tralee to investigate themselves and that "Due to an administrative error the file had gone missing"

The coincidences were now piling up.

Sleep is the most basic thing we do, we need it and it gets us ready for the next day, if we don't get it strange things happen to the body. I wasn't sleeping, how could i? Everything was going over and over in my mind and it didn't make sense.

I contacted Solicitors for a Judicial Review of the findings and was asked for €10,000 upfront so i couldn't do that. Shockingly in Ireland you don't have access to the courts when you need them unless you have money. I then contacted every TD and sent the damning documents against the state and again no-one replied. I then contacted almost every journalist in Ireland (also RTE Primetime) with my proof and again no one wanted to know. One of RTE's biggest reporters just blocked me and the Court Journalist who appeared on TV on the documentary (the guy who clearly loved it) also blocked me and sent me a rejection letter an hour later from a job application i sent him the previous year. I then contacted Liveline, my only hope and they said they "weren't interested" They also said it was "Too Complicated".

No one wanted to know, the papers who wrote all those lies about me historically didn't want to know or help in any way and so my gut wrenching stress continued to rise.

Over the next 3 years i came back to Ireland from Greece and Portugal to Kerry and Clare and was getting stopped and searched with sirens and lights by Gardai, i've been interrogated in Supermarkets, pulled out of taxis, followed by Garda Cars and lost jobs. Now again i have to stress that these are good Gardai who don't know the background and are only doing there job by acting on what they remember from PULSE.

The real Conman was eventually convicted and sentenced but got away with it for much longer as i was in the frame and being watched. Iv'e been evicted from houses in Ireland as recently as April 2020 during the Corona Virus and was left in an awful situation. Each time i made a complaint to GSOC and each time they turned it down without looking at CCTV or more and they just said the same thing every time "Superintendent ...... found no evidence of intelligence being compiled about you by Garda X and therefore you cannot be harassed by the state" In my calls to GSOC i was being constantly made out to be a liar and by one officer KD in particular (i have recordings) They are not as independent as they make themselves out to be.

Last year in Ireland i landed a role with an Irish Online Station, it seemed like a big one and i'd watched it for a long time so we decided to team up with a new morning show and aim for the FM licence. Myself and my Global Sponsor spent months arranging the equipment we would need and they sent over €3000 worth of Studio equipment to Ireland from Australia for my show. I even got a Studio in Kenmare in Kerry and contacted artists and more planning the show. It got some traction in the media in Ireland, but as per usual out of the blue one day i got the dreaded email to say someone emailed him about Google and that "I won't get advertisers or Insurance" for the station because of me and so it wasn't going to happen" That was a shock and very embarrassing because he then contacted the Newspapers to have the articles removed which they did.

I don't know what he said but those papers have not supported me since. I have heard since that his station has upset an established Irish Station by continently using it's tagline to attract listeners and i'm glad now i'm not with it.

As usual i had to move on.

Now remember that for 3 years GSOC refused to take me seriously and kept referring to the findings of the Superintendent in 2017. That I made it all up and was never shows those records....

However in November 2019 GSOC contacted me in Portugal to tell me they were opening a "Public interest investigation" into my being given Garda Intelligence" from someone.

So now I WAS given it, but rather than punish the Superintendent for misleading them for 3 years they just forgot about it.

I again contacted the Irish Media with this very damning letter which contradicted totally the Garda Superintendent's one in 2017 but no one wanted to know. I then got a letter from GSOC in reply to my asking for a review based on this new information and it said, "the day they decided to launch the Public Interest Investigation for the Gardai they decided not to review my case from 2017" signed KD.

Now i wanted to scream!

In Ireland people know that the state has made shocking mistakes in the past, the problem is that they don't ever admit to it until after they have been found out.

When i think about Garda X i cannot understand his actions, not only did he destroy my life but he was willing to throw his Garda colleague (The Whistleblower) under a bus to save himself. He also had his superiors set out to discredit me to GSOC to make it all go away (which it did). I don't think i will ever get over this emotionally, and the absolute wall of silence i have met through media, politicians and more. It has caused me countless sleepless nights and resulted in my relationship ending. Now i know some people will doubt what i have said here thinking surely the state wouldn't do that? It's a powerful entity, look back at recent Irish history and see how many things it covered up and the good people it tried to destroy. In saying that, look at the good is has done. Balance is very important in life, there are bad but there are more good!

To this day other than that Garda Superintendent and higher Police ranks in Kerry, no one from GSOC or any other state body has forensically looked at Garda X's Pulse file to see that he did indeed compile all that evidence in 2017. He destroyed me and my hard work and had it covered up by a superior who mislead GSOC.

Sadly he and his superiors were only starting with me and i'll get back to this later with a new development.

16. Awards and the Algarve

In March 2018 i was offered a Gig DJing in an Irish bar in the Algarve in Portugal, it was in Alvor, i loved it, and i was now broadcasting my online "breaking show" from there. The bar is a perfect Irish bar ran by 2 Dublin men and they made me feel so welcome. The radio show went again from strength to strength and by now Z1 was 1MUSIC, i restarted the station and called it 1MUSIC. From the start it was hard as the Radio News Website in Ireland "Radio Today" tweeted that it "looks like a blatant copy of Apple Beats1 to us" which humiliated me from the get go. I threatened legal action and told them my station was there before Beats1 and they then deleted the tweet. By now they knew who i was from sending them updates and like everyone else they were focusing on the old fake stories and so had no interest. Everyone always assumed that i was making these things up but they never checked.

I persevered, and sent a demo to a big station in Portugal. I then kept doing my own show and in May 2018 was nominated as a finalist on the MORA Radio Awards. Now this is big, the MORAS are ran my Mixcloud and that year they were open to every station in the World and every Dj wether on Mixcloud or not. I was nominated and for the first time in 5 Years a positive story was now on Google.

Word got around Ireland and i started to get good feedback, this was new to me! Now every time someone would put it on Social Media it was always inevitable that some troll would post the worst link possible as the reply and that i wasn't to be believed, it was up and down for weeks!

I was given a job on the Radio Station in Portugal, they had created a New Afternoon Slot for me from Midday to

4pm Monday-Friday, WOW! I had made it! I was speechless.

I was now on FM Radio in Portugal.

The following day it appeared on 1 Irish Paper that i was now on this well known station on FM in Portugal in the beautiful Algarve. It was then on a Portuguese Newspaper and I had finally made it! Good news was now online and I had my and any Radio Dj's dream job. But then i was scared, i had told the station about the problems I was having and i knew the trolls would not be happy, i was right.

The Friday before my first show on this dream station i received a text message, it was awful, worse than awful, it said "Congratulations on the ...FM job you C*NT, now, if you don't pay me €1000 into my PayPal in the next 24hrs (he gave it) i will send every presenter you work with and everyone connected with the station all the bad google stuff about you, there are better Dj's out there that deserve that job" I was gutted and now scared, i couldn't lose this job and so i paid it.

The first day on the station was so cool, I was in my element and everything else did not matter from Midday to 4pm Monday to Friday, all the problems i had just disappeared when that microphone went on, i loved it. I then got a job in one of the Algarve's biggest Clubs and was working there 6 nights a week as well as being on the radio, i had a lovely apartment and although i was lonely, life was good.

A few days later we were doing an outside broadcast in the Algarve. It was a stunningly beautiful day and i was broadcasting my Radio show from Zoomarine, what an experience that was. I think out of every radio experience i ever had that one will remain. I remember watching the dolphin show before i went on air and getting emotional at it all. Just a perfect perfect day. Life was good and i started to cry. I freshened up and went On- air in 30degrees heat in the most incredible surroundings. For a moment it all sank in and i smiled to myself. I hadn't done that in a long time.

My show was almost over and then the News came, it was big News, it was HUGE.

The message came through that i had won the award and was now "World's Number 1 Pop Music Show "

It was the proudest moment of my life, i persevered, i never gave up, i took the punches and kept getting up and it paid off. Not only did i win the Award by the Industry Judges but i also got another award from the listeners Vote. I was now in the Irish Mirror and Joe.ie, the Sunday World had 2 full positive pages about "my redemption story" thanks to Eamon Dillon, what a headline! People were now starting to see how hard i was actually working. Over the next few months things got even more surreal, in a studio with the fabulous Cliff Richard and Bonnie Tyler, doing outside broadcasts from The Portugal Golf Masters, my listen backs to my shows were now at 50k plus per show! I am the most streamed Irish Radio Dj of the last two years still. Yet something was niggling away at me. The same Irish Papers that destroyed me were still ignoring me and refusing to write about my achievements? Why? Even my award wasn't mentioned on the Radio News site in Ireland but the other winners were.

It wasn't that i had an ego, i never had, it was that i needed positive stories online to get the bad ones down that were damaging me. To be fair by now some papers had removed old stories when i asked them as it was clear i had moved on. Others didn't.

That year i met Noel Baker from the Irish Examiner in Cork, now it was my time, we spoke at length for hours and then parted ways. I like Noel, he's a decent Journalist and a nice guy, he had written a story about me in 2011 but was now willing to give an update, now that's good journalism, balance. Months came and went and i was working hard on the Radio, i was living the radio dream. Now it was bizarre, i was famous and well liked in Portugal and when i went back to Ireland i was getting stopped by some Gardai and interrogated as to where i was going, again only doing their jobs by recalling what they saw on Pulse. It was crazy!

All this time i was losing friends bit by bit in the Algarve, it was clear by now that rumours were being spread about me on Google by someone very very close to me with an agenda, and i was starting to lose my credibility and friends. It turns out someone I worked with was sharing the old Google links to people.

It's sad as he knew well what I've been through. The same guy is always on Social Media looking for sympathy and talking about mental health issues.

Some people..

There was still no sign of Noel's article (not his fault) and so i reached out to another from a major UK paper as i needed balance quickly online. The journalist flew over and met me and that Sunday i was in The

Sunday Times UK with the headline "NO MORE CRIMINAL RECORDS" it was just what i needed, now people would see the truth and where i was in my life and my achievement, wow! I was so happy and i settled down for the best night sleep ever....or so i thought.

11pm Sunday night my phone alert

went off a few times which was odd, i looked at it and people in the Algarve were tagging me on an article on an English owned Algarve Daily News Site, one was messaging me that "If i was you i'd get out of Portugal quick" and then it turned racist, it was seriously intense, what was going on? I clicked to see what i was being tagged on and what is saw shocked and hurt me so much that it made me walk away from my dream Radio job on the Afternoon Show.

(Station Named) DJ IS IRELAND'S GREATEST CONMAN

No, No No, What?? It went on to tell all about the "crimes". It went into detail about my depression and made it out to be something awful and humiliated me in the worst possible way, it said i was psychotic, it was awful. It said i was there hiding under the identity of Frankie Beats (my Dj name since i was 15) it questioned all my achievements and recent interviews and then said that there would now be a European Arrest Warrant now that "they" knew where i was.

I had been through so much and had so many knocks but this was bad, my reputation was in tatters and i was getting abuse now from people at 11pm over a horrible article that just copied and pasted the old and fake articles and put opinion pieces in between. Not once did the Journalist/Owner contact me first for a "Right of Reply" It was a complete hatchet job that destroyed all my hard work. If he had researched he would have seen how hard i was working and my awards and more, he would have seen that there is 11 days owed for on of the sentences from 2006 which only came to light recently and is going through the proper channels to be removed. There never was or is a European Warrant and iv'e been working my arse off for the last 10 years.

He just wanted an extreme headline and he destroyed my hard work and career. My boss phoned me around midnight, was i okay she said, i told her i was leaving the station as i was humiliated. She persuaded me over the next hour to do my show as normal as people would be listening tomorrow and if i wasn't on they would assume it was all true and so i went and done my show as normal. She's a wonderful woman and she has helped my career so much in the last few years.

The abuse was relentless, people were talking about me, that evening i went for dinner in Albufeira and an English woman stood up and told people all about me and that i was a conman, she said there was a European warrant for me, i was mortified and made the decision i was going home. I had enough. I gave my notice to the Station and left. It was the hardest thing i ever had to do, i didn't deserve that to happen to me, it was wrong in every way and journalism at it's worst.

My dream job that I had worked so hard for, I was now giving it up.

To be fair to the paper thankfully they deleted the piece but for me the damage was done and all again because of old, fake, out of context and one sided Google stories and it cost me my dream.

I was finished !

17. Ireland

I was now back in Ireland and unemployed with no hope of work anywhere, i had reached the highs and each time was dragged back down in an extreme way and always over Google.

I met my ex girlfriend and i decided i was going to do my best and get her back. I applied for every job i could think off and other than have another fall i told them everything about me in the initial email.

Out of the blue i received a call from a hotel owner in Munster. He liked my story and wanted to meet me at the hotel. Now this was a big deal, it was as if life was giving me a second chance.

A few days later i met him at the hotel and we spoke for ages about my life and experience and he brought up my past first, all signs were good. By now Noel had pushed to get my article out as i think maybe he was frustrated with the Portugal story also. I gave the hotelier the Irish Examiner to read as i was proud of their full page story about me and a few days later i was offered the job. I was happy and even thought foolishly that maybe myself and my ex would get back together, looking back at it, it was a selfish thought. She was after all better off without me and she deserved the best in life after what i put her through.

Now i'm not going to go into too much here as sadly this is the subject of a "Criminal Complaint" let me explain briefly. I got taxis to and from work very day and worked hard to get the hotel ready for opening , i was bringing boxes of work home with me but i didn't mind as this was my way back into Ireland.

After a few weeks i noticed i wasn't getting any money and there was no sign of it coming so i gave my notice to the Hotel along with a detailed email outlining all i had done for them. I then was offered work back in Greece, now if you haven't noticed already, Greece has been good to me, it's my spiritual home and always will be, when i am there i fell utter peace and i love it. While i was in Greece working i didn't feel right, i kept thinking about how close i was to potentially getting my relationship back and now i had gone running from Google again so maybe i should just focus on doing the right thing for her.

I text the hotelier and told him if he wanted to start again i would come back and he said "okay" when you're back in Ireland message me. Again things felt good and so i left Greece and flew back to Ireland to get my job back.

I met the hotelier along with his number 2 and the Hotel General Manager, he had a great team to be fair but when he saw me initially that day his reaction was strange, he was stand offish and seemed angry, but i thought maybe he was just "being the boss" and i brushed it off.

The meeting was good, i apologised for

leaving but explained why i did it. In the conversation they said they needed to see i was serious this time and wouldn't leave again and so i promised to find a house in the area and cancel any gigs i had all summer long and focus on the hotel. They all agreed and i was due to start Thursday physically at the hotel as it opened. After the meeting i found a small cafe and i made call after call and eventually got a Long Term house by chance and phoned the venues in Kerry to cancel my bookings. I was focused. I felt hope sitting in the cafe looking at the ocean, absolute hope.

The day before i was due to start i got the house, i moved in and felt stable for the first time in a long time, this was different as it was Ireland and it was where it all started back in 2000. This was me being accepted as a person and not a past. That night i received a text to say the Number 2 was sick and to "take the day off" which i did, but the following day i received another text, this time to say the job was gone. What? I had cancelled everything, flown back from Greece and got a house and now this?

I telephoned the owner and i was upset, he told me someone else had come back to work (which i knew was a lie) i then asked him for €100 at least as i was after getting a house and had now no work. He laughed at me and said "I'm not responsible for you" before hanging up.

I can't tell you how much i cried over the last few years, i can't because i'm utterly ashamed to tell you all the times i did. That night alone in a house i now couldn't pay for and with €15 in my pocket i was hysterical. I'd given up my contract in Greece and gigs in Ireland, i was used and treated shockingly. I broke down and i cried and cried and cried. A few days later for the first time in 10 years i was back on medication for depression over the Hotelier.

Over the next few months i picked myself up and had got back to Portugal and started back in the Clubs and slowly back on the Radio, every week i would send the hotelier an email asking for wages i was owed or at least an apology. It was a matter of principle now, he had used me to get the hotel ready, but he never replied. On principle i wasn't letting it go, as it now totally finished any chance of my relationship being repaired. Remember, he knew of my problems and struggles and used me knowing he could drop me by using that at any stage. In August i stopped emailing as he wasn't replying and i moved on.

It was now November 2019, and an article appeared in The Sunday Times UK about GSOC opening the public interest investigation. This was the first time the Garda X incident was now public. A few days later i received a call from Tralee to say that my apartment was after being raided by Gardai with a Search Warrant. They were looking for my phone and laptop. The Gardai were based in a station that was subject of 2 of my GSOC complaints. Someone in that Station had giving information to a potential employer of mine in 2016 and another one was them following me through another town in 2019 for an hour and calling my landlord and got me evicted. Both cases were (like the rest) thrown out by GSOC.

I had sent them again CCTV info and more and none was looked at. Again they said that i wasn't being harassed as the Superintendent in 2017 found no intelligence compiled about me by Garda X. I was taken aback as to why a search warrant would be executed on me in Tralee by Gardai from another county? It turns out they were looking for my laptop and phone, the same phone i took the call from the Whistleblower on. A coincidence of course but it would be easy to assume otherwise.

I telephoned the Gardai in Tralee and spoke to a very nice Detective there who whilst he couldn't tell me what it was about kinda nudged me in the right direction and gave me the name of the Investigating Garda.

The Garda eventually called me back, at this stage i was back in Portugal, he told me the hotelier had accused me of harassing him, i was now very angry, how dare he, he done me wrong. The Garda said I needed to make a statement about it and so i told him I would come back immediately to Ireland to clear my name. I cancelled my work and flew back days later to Ireland and arrived to Tralee, by now it was almost Christmas and I again was not sleeping as my mind was going over everything that's happened over the years and now i had this to deal with and i was very lonely.

I phoned the Garda and told him i would be at his Police Station in a few days, he said no, he wanted to meet me in Tralee Police station. This wasn't good, i explained my issues with the Superintendent there over the Garda X incident (he was now based permanently in Tralee) and the Sunday previous the Sunday Times article appeared about Garda X in Tralee. Friday came and i went to Tralee Garda Station at 9am, i was so anxious, of all stations i did not want to be here but i wanted to clear my name so i had to. The 2 detectives arrived and to my absolute shock i was immediately arrested and placed in a cell.

Think about all i have been though, all the ups and downs and i never gave up. All the hard work i had done over the years was now for nothing. All i wanted to do was do the right thing and show people the real me and here i was in a cell in a police station in Tralee where my complaint about Garda X was and where the Superintendent was based who investigated my complaints and had said "i made it up". I was questioned for hours and it became clear that the hotelier hadn't told them everything, he told them he didn't know about my past and that i was lying. I explained about the full page Irish Examiner Newspaper i gave him and the fact that from the start he knew, and that he had spoken to references who also told him. The Garda whilst very nice and professional just didn't seem to believe me.

They showed me a bank statement belonging to me and my Portuguese Tax details, they had taken them during the search in Tralee. The bank statement was under the name Frank Regan. Now i had changed my name officially years previous but told no-one, it was the only thing that gave me peace, when i was Frankie Shanley i was having an awful time over the Intelligence from 2017. I was being shot down on every occasion i used ID because now and then someone would Google me. Then for some reason they would call the Gardai and my world would come crashing down. I wasn't trying to hide, i was trying to have a normal life. When i became Frank Regan it stopped. But now Frank Regan was on the Pulse Garda System.

It was clear the Gardai were assuming i had done something illegal to have that statement. It's always been "Assumptions". I was eventually released after 7pm and again the 2 Gardai were professional and courteous. All of the extension to my detention in Tralee and more were all signed by the Superintendent who was the one from my GSOC complaint, this was not a coincidence.

At the time of writing this it has now come to light that i am to be charged over emailing the hotelier looking for wages and an apology. Of all the valid complaints i have made over the years of people harassing me, nothing every happened. Even the one about Garda X "Disappeared". This event has made me realise that there is no point anymore in me trying in Ireland.

I was eventually released and signed my papers to go, i was burned out by now and it was late. But as i was released the real reason i was in Tralee came to light. I noticed another official looking Garda waiting for me, He was an inspector and rather than be released i was then further detained, this time over Garda X and the intelligence. This was the real reason it was Tralee. I was questioned about who gave me the intelligence. These 2 officers were extremely professional and polite. All over that

Superintendent lying to protect his Garda and now trying another angle to get at me.

I was fingerprinted and photographed again and released with documents all signed by the Garda Superintendent who led the GSOC case.

A few weeks later i was Djing in a venue in Cork that i love and on leaving the venue at 2:30am was stopped outside by another 2 Detectives and again questioned about what Garda gave me the information, but this time i got the "This isn't going to go away" comment.

Too many coincidences by now, and remember that i was the victim here of malicious Garda intelligence.

In June 2020 i moved back to Greece, COVID had changed the world and yet here was i working 7 nights a week on a Greek island. It may sound nice but i'm extremely lonely. Everyone is with their family and loved ones afraid of this unknown virus and here i am trying to stay focused by working abroad. I'm risking my health to take my mind off things in Ireland and reluctant to return over my continuing harassment over Garda X.

Let's talk about Greece, as i said it's my home. When things have been bad i have always came here to find myself and recharge. The country itself is stunningly beautiful and the people are so welcoming. One thing that stands out in Corfu are the cats, they are everywhere and they just add to the calmness of the island. Greece or Portugal never cared about my historical issues, they cared about me now and my journey. They welcomed me with open arms and accepted me despite my flaws, and in my times of utter despair and sadness they probably saved me.

It was 6pm on a hot Tuesday afternoon in July Corfu, i had been told that an

Inspector in Tralee was looking to speak to me and so i rang the station to leave my number with the hope that there was a development with my Garda X case. The phone rang and it was the Inspector.

Emotions were setting in, i felt an overwhelming sense of hope in an instant, i assumed there were positive developments...i was wrong.

The inspector told me that i am to meet him in Ireland to formally be questioned in relation to Garda X.

Garda X had made a statement to his superiors saying that i was harassing him since 2017 through GSOC cases.

Read that piece again...

The Garda who absolutely destroyed me in 2017, the Garda who insinuated i was involved in a crime, the Garda who had his Superiors delete/hide/cover up Intelligence on Pulse when he was found out, the Garda who caused me to lose my home, job, business, relationship of 15yrs and cause me to be harassed for 4 years.

The Garda who i complained about in 2017 in a Garda Station in Tullamore over him harassing me which was then sent to Tralee and then "Due to an administrative error the file had disappeared" was now saying that i was harassing HIM.

Why did his superiors not pull him aside and say to him it was not worth it? Why they didn't say it's too risky as all Frankie's FOI documents will be made public in court as will the whole story. Everything will come out publicly that has happened me and Garda X and his Superior will look bad and open themselves to an investigation and more.

Now remember that i was the victim of all this in 2017. I am still suffering over him, more nightmares, more sleepless nights, more stress.

I claimed (and could prove) harassment from him and here i am now with 2 harassment cases pending against me. Payback

But again, it won't change my mind about Irish Police being the best! They are, and i still have respect for the decent men and women who put on the uniform to protect each and every one of us professionally for little money. In recent days one of the Gardai from a case in 2005 helped me with a matter back in Ireland. He prosecuted me back then and like most was very fair. I remembered him and called him from Greece, he did everything to help me and the matter was sorted within 24hrs.

Policing at it's best from West Cork!

I have again sent another complaint to the Garda Commissioner (attached at the end of the book) and to GSOC over

Garda X's decision to complain about me and have me arrested. I'm expecting the usual dropping of the case from GSOC but i hope the Commissioner will now finally help seeing that it is evident something is not right.

I will be arrested/questioned in Tralee Garda station with the Garda Superintendent i have been complaining about on duty and his officers questioning me.. That's wrong.

18. Looking Back..

I often look back on that date when i drove to that Garda Station, i often think what if didn't hand myself up, so many what ifs'. I've learned a lot about myself in all of this, i've learned especially that i'm stronger than i think. I'm well aware that most people will say i deserved it all, but really?

I hate night time when the lights go out, i hate that part of the day. I dread the night. I put on Frasier or Seinfeld on repeat at night and it stops my thinking for a little bit and hopefully i'll fall asleep.

That's why i wrote this book, it's not for fame, or showing off, or to make money, it's to finally tell my real story.

In January 2020 Al Jazeera invited me on as a panelist to it's almost 40 Million viewers to tell my story and it felt great. Yet in Ireland i've always been doubted and not believed because when people read the historic headlines they assume i'm lying. When i started on the big FM Radio Station in Portugal the station was getting messages from people in Ireland saying that "He's Ireland's Greatest Conman and his name is Frankie Shanley not Frankie Beats"

My First few months on the Station

were an emotional nightmare, i was terrified waiting for the next fire i would have to put out and i loved my life there. At least 8 times in my first few months i flew back to Ireland as i was feeling the pressure and each time i came back it would always end up with another GSOC complaint over harassment and a few days later the inevitable "not proceeding with the investigation" email from GSOC.

It was tough.

I could go on and on but i won't. And i have so much more I could have wrote here, but i won't.

Please remember, i'm not here to bash Gardai, I have nothing but respect for them, we are so lucky in Ireland to have a fantastic Police force, they put on the uniform day in and out to risk their lives for us. They are utterly professional and polite. And remember, it was a good Garda that risked his job to reach out to me in early 2017. The majority of them couldn't have been nicer including the ones who took my statement in 2015. I remember some gave me phone calls home from court cells to relax me as I was distressed and others even brought me food when i wasn't getting any from the Prison movements. Things they did not have to do.

Prison officers, they were also good (especially the kitchen staff) and they have a horrible job to do. They helped me get through this all more than they will ever know and i cannot thank them enough.

Journalists, i've met fantastic ones and editors too, ones who cared and pushed to give me the balanced update that i needed.

GSOC, i can safely say i will never contact them again for anything, they are pointless and in the end caused me more stress and sleepless nights than

Garda X did. They just didn't believe me over the Superintendent sending them my convictions and FOI docs will show that "Google him" was also used in the GSOC office. Garda X is now Garda Sergeant X. In time someone will get access to their Pulse entries and they will get what they deserve.

Who knows, maybe this book will force someone to act to help me, but i seriously doubt that.

Now let's me realistic, there are people reading this saying it's a consequence for what i did do? I've paid way, way more than what i should have, the maximum sentence was 12-24 months and by now i have spent over 7 years in Prison which is the equivalent of an 11 year sentence (before remission) since making that statement in 2005 and mostly for crimes I did not commit. And i am still paying for it this very day.

In general i have learned that there are 2

strands of justice in Ireland, one for the wealthy who use the high court as a playpen for little things and then the strand that deals with normal people who don't stand a chance in it and get chewed up.

It all created the me that people have based everything on for the last 15 years whilst not knowing the real story..until now. And yes i did commit crimes back then, i have nothing but shame and regret about that. I was not myself, and committed a small percentage of what i was eventually convicted off on that drip feed basis over the years. I also have to be clear that i'm not taking away from the seriousness of any crime.

The report from the independent Psychologist who was on my side was tough to read, it showed with evidence what the state were doing and no judge would have sentenced me based on just that. It was clear something was seriously wrong, but because of the manner in which i was charged in court it could never used but Professor HK's (state psychologist's) one always was.

Since the incident with Garda X in 2017 my life changed in Ireland and i was afraid to go outside most of the time. Garda X made a serious error of judgement or intentionally tried to damage me over the failed case, either way what happened after made it worse.

Everything i have said in this book i can back up with official state papers, from my extreme movements in Prison to the TB cover up documents from the State's own computer system , the documents from Prof HK saying "Stop all meds" and he "Never was sick" to the 2 contradictory letters from GSOC, one saying the Garda X intelligence never happened and 3 years later saying it probably did, and all the state papers that have been ignored by the authorities and TD's and Solicitors.

I have wrote numerous times to the Taoiseach, the Garda Commissioner and the Minster of Justice with the proof of everything about the Garda X incident. The new Garda Commissioner replied with a reference number to say that an investigation had started but that was it. The Taoiseach's office sent generic replies and someone from the Minister of Justice's office recently sent me an email telling me to "Contact GSOC"

Now? My New Music Playlists are Number 1 on Spotify in Ireland and Portugal (non

Spotify branded) and my shows have been listened back to over 300,000 times in 2 years on Mixcloud. I now get retweets from the likes of Dj Khaled, Bishop Briggs, the Seinfeld cast and more. Iv'e interviewed some big artists and gained respect in the Music industry abroad. Social Media was my only way of showing people what i was doing and that i was successful in my field but also made life hard for me from the trolls. It probably made them think i was bragging and so made them angry, but it was my only way of showing my detractors and everyone else that i was working hard and doing amazing things.

In the last few months a small station launched in I clearly using a play on my 1MUSIC name. I started legal proceedings against the former RTE 2FM Dj who started it. It became the most stressful few months ever with personal attack after personal attack from him. When i saw the station had 12 listeners one weekend i knew it was not worth the drama and so i backed off.

Besides everything that has happened i still haven't lost my sense of wonder and often sit down and look at the stars like i did all those years ago. I can't stress how good people can be. In the last few months i have started to receive support from Ireland especially from the

Irish Times and it is overwhelming to say the least. In Jan 2021 i was responsible for the Garda Jerusalema dance challenge. Whilst the likes of a radio station in Mayo deleted the story when they saw it was me behind it, others have not and have praised me. I lifted the nation when it needed it but I have also decided never to return to it. Now as you know i've had 2 main "Trolls" a radio dj in Portugal and a radio dj in Sligo Ireland. Police in Portugal have started full criminal proceedings against my UK Radio troll based here who hounded me but in Ireland i'm told it's a civil matter and not a Police one (no surprise there)

If you take anything from this book it's this.. Never give up.

No matter how bad things are, no matter how much the weight of the world is on your shoulders, DON'T give up. Stay positive and focus on whatever small thing makes you happy, never ever lose hope.

I now live between Greece and the Algarve Portugal. Life is good, but I do utterly miss my ex girlfriend to this day and have nothing but regret for that and what I put her through.

I've been very lucky, or do I deserve it? I'm almost afraid to think the latter.

By writing this book i can finally tell people what really happened and that in itself has been the reason in writing it. As I said it's not to make money or be famous or to get sympathy.

The ultimate goal is to finally get the the one thing I have not had in a very very long time..

A good nights sleep. Thanks for reading

To view some of the State documents:

https://tinyurl.com/5a4mgoyu

ABOUT THE AUTHOR

Frankie Beats is a Radio Dj in Portugal. He is 43 and originally from Roscommon Ireland. In 2018 he won the award for Number 1 Pop Music Radio show in the World.

Printed in Great Britain
by Amazon